OUR
GREAT AND
AWESOME
GOD

OUR GREAT AND AWESOME GOD

Meditations For Athletes

Elliot Johnson
AND Al Schierbaum

Wolgemuth & Hyatt, Publishers, Inc.
Brentwood, Tennessee

© 1989 by Elliot Johnson and Al Schierbaum. All rights reserved
Published April 1990. First Edition
Printed in the United States of America
97 96 95 94 93 92 91 90   8 7 6 5 4 3 2 (Second printing, August 1990)

Wolgemuth & Hyatt, Publishers, Inc.
1749 Mallory Lane, Suite 110, Brentwood, Tennessee 37027.

Library of Congress Cataloging-in-Publication Data

Johnson, Elliot.
    Our great and awesome God : meditations for athletes / Elliot
Johnson and Al Schierbaum. — 1st ed.
        p. cm.
    ISBN 0-943497-84-1
    1. Athletes — Prayer-books and devotions — English.   2. Meditations.
I. Schierbaum, Al. II. Title.
BV4596.A8J64   1990
242'.68 — dc20   90-31635
                                                                                      CIP

Dedicated to
"God, the Blessed and only Ruler,
the King of kings and Lord of lords,
who alone is immortal and who lives in
unapproachable light,
whom no one has seen or can see.
To Him be honor and might forever."
(1 Timothy 6:15–16)

CONTENTS

FOREWORD

The authors of this book are not pastors or seminary professors. We will not waste time debating mundane issues that God has not revealed to man in the first place. We are baseball coaches — rivals on the athletic field and in the recruiting wars. We compete with one another. But in our spirits we are one, for both of us have been found by a Head Coach who loves us, and we have eagerly "signed a blank contract" to play for Him forever! The pact has been secured by the blood of His wonderful Son — Jesus Christ — and sealed by His Holy Spirit. This Spirit, who indwells us, is His down payment and is a fantastic gift! Furthermore, when this earthly life is over, the eternal rewards are *out of this world*!

When student athletes are considering a college or university, the first thing they want to know about is the nature of the head coach. What is he really like? How does he treat his players? What are the purposes and objectives of his program? They discover facts about the coach both before they sign scholarship papers and after they have made the commitment to attend the school. The nature of the head coach is the single most important aspect of the athlete's athletic experience.

In the spiritual realm, the knowledge of our heavenly Father is the most important information we can pursue. What is *He* like? How does *He* treat *His* players? What are *His* purposes and objectives? We discover some things about Him before we trust His Son as Savior and much more after committing our lives to Him. By learning how He feels about issues, we discover what our reactions should be. By knowing Him more deeply, we are better able to recognize counterfeits who claim to represent Him.

He is an awesome God! He is a wonderful heavenly Father! It is a privilege to play on His team! Let us introduce you to our Head Coach! We do not know everything about Him, but the more we discover, the more excited we become! We know He will never disappoint anyone who sincerely wants to know Him.

Elliot Johnson & Al Schierbaum

INTRODUCTION

American sports fans lavish their heroes with words of praise. The word *awesome* has been used to describe a Michael Jordan slam dunk, a Dwight Gooden fastball, or a bone-crushing tackle by Lawrence Taylor. The athletic achievements of the stars become our topics of conversation, and the exploits often become our centers of attention.

Webster's dictionary defines *awe* as a "feeling of fearful or profound respect or wonder inspired by greatness, superiority, grandeur, etc. of a person or thing and suggests an immobilizing effect." This description only fits the God of the universe and His achievements! Our God is an awesome God! No one can fathom His greatness (Psalms 145:3). No study of God can be comprehensive. He is too big for pen and ink to describe. But as we focus attention upon Him, our problems diminish in proportion. So let us study who He is and what He does. Let us get to know Him, not because of what He has, but because of who He *is!*

To know God is the greatest goal anyone could ever set. This was the goal of the Apostle Paul, who said that he considered "everything a loss compared to the surpassing greatness of *knowing* Christ Jesus my Lord" (Philippians 3:8, emphasis added). The Lord Jesus Himself said, "This is life eternal, that they might *know* you, the only true God, and

Jesus Christ, whom you have sent" (John 17:3, emphasis added). What is eternal life? It is knowing God! In Jeremiah 9:23–24, the Lord says, "Let not the wise man boast of his wisdom or the strong man boast of his riches, but let him who boasts boast about this: that he understands and *knows* me, that I am the Lord who exercises kindness, justice, and righteousness on earth, for in these I delight" (emphasis added). What brings delight to God? It is our knowledge and understanding of Him!

We will study the attributes of God—those qualities of God which constitute what He is. They are the very characteristics of His nature. The attributes of God are not the works of God, but the very nature of God. It is the nature of God to produce *infinite* works. What God has done is simply proof of who He is!

Though we will be treating each attribute separately, they are all interrelated, without conflict, working together. Love, power, holiness, and knowledge are all attributes of God. His love is holy, and His power is governed by His knowledge, love and holiness. Though there are many qualities that make up our personalities, we are still one person; so it is with God. He is complex. All His attributes are perfect, and they work together perfectly.

It is impossible to define God. But we must think accurately about Him, for if we are mistaken about His nature, we will be mistaken about the nature of man, of sin, of the world, and of salvation. Though many believe wrong things about God, we must recognize Him as Lord and King of the universe. God is absolutely wonderful, and, after learning of Him, none of us will have any excuse not to trust Him!

PART 1

THE NATURE
OF GOD

GOD EXISTS

Read Genesis 1   *In the beginning God . . .*
                                                    (Genesis 1:1)

U ntil his retirement in May of 1989, Mike Schmidt was a
great ball player. During nearly two decades with the
Philadelphia Phillies, Mike hit 548 home runs and won ten
Golden Glove awards as a defensive player! No other third
baseman performed with both bat and glove the way Mike
performed. He had nothing more to prove to anyone on the
baseball field. Mike Schmidt was simply a Hall of Fame
player.

Just as Mike Schmidt has no more to prove, our Lord has
nothing more to prove to anyone in this world either. He certainly is under no obligation to any of His creation to prove
either His existence or any attribute of His wonderful nature!

It is God's nature to exist. The Bible (Genesis 1:1) assumes the existence of God before creation. There was never a
time when God did not exist. No one needs to *prove* His existence, and He is not obligated to prove it to anyone. He simply *is!* He had no beginning, and He will have no end. No one
caused Him to exist or brought Him into existence, for God is
the "Uncaused One."

God is completely self-sufficient. He is dependent upon no
one. He doesn't need you, me, or any other part of His cre-

ation to continue to exist as God. Man is dependent upon God, the Giver of Life. Man is dependent upon the biological resources God gives us (water, air, and food) to survive. Man is also dependent upon other men for support and help. In contrast, God needs nothing to stay alive. It is simply His nature to live. 1 Thessalonians 1:9 says that God is the living and true God. John 5:26 says that God has life within Himself. Daniel 6:26–27 tells that His kingdom endures forever. Jesus said, "I am the way, the truth, and the life" (John 14:6). When Jesus speaks of giving life, He is not speaking of physical existence, but of union with God. To "plug into God," the Source of life, is to gain eternal life. Eternal life means a life of purpose, activity, vitality, and satisfaction. Anything short of a life with God is a cheap substitute for true life. What a tremendous privilege: to know this awesome God!

Furthermore, God is not a rewarder of those who only believe that He *exists*. The demons believe He exists! God is a rewarder of those who *diligently* seek Him (Hebrews 11:6) and of those who believe that He is a God of provision (Matthew 6:25–33). He rewards those who believe He is the Lord of all! He rewards those who trust Him for salvation. In Isaiah 45:22, God says, "Turn to me and be saved . . . for I am God and there is no other."

Only a fool would deny that Mike Schmidt was a highly skilled ball player with Hall of Fame credentials. And only a fool would deny God's existence, His power, and His authority over mankind. Psalms 14:1 records, "The fool says in his heart, 'There is no God.' " A fool not only denies the existence of God, but he also denies the control, provision, and care of God in this world. To deny that God is actively involved in His creation is to deny the very nature of God. Sometimes people who claim to be Christians live as atheists, not trusting God for their lives and for His control in the affairs of the world. Titus 1:16 says, "They profess to know

God, but by their deeds [life style] they deny Him"(NAS). Many are infected with a touch of atheism, because (experientially) they doubt the sovereignty of a holy and wonderful God in their lives. How shameful to deny His goodness and His care! Our Father deserves much better from His creatures!

In each situation we encounter, we must consciously realize that God does exist. May each of us never fail to trust Him.

Meditation Time-Out

1. Meditate upon the fact that God has always existed.

2. Meditate upon the fact that God is completely sufficient within Himself.

3. Note the vast differences between yourself and God by listing the things upon which you depend for existence and enjoyment in life. Imagine what you would be like if you had need of none of these things.

4. Have you been made one with God through Jesus Christ so you can truly experience life?

   • If yes, when and how did it happen?

   • If no, bow before Him right now, confess your sin and separation from Him, and ask Him to come into your life. He will give you new life and a new nature!

5. Are you a professing Christian but a practicing atheist?

   • Do you trust God with each detail of your life?

   • If not, why not?

   • Remember, you have no *good* reason not to trust God.

GOD IS SPIRIT

Read Colossians 1:15–20

God is spirit, and his worshipers must worship in spirit and in truth.

(John 4:24)

A generation ago, Dodger outfielder Pete Reiser was known as a talented athlete who played with great enthusiasm. He was constantly leaping, diving, and sliding, often injuring himself by crashing into walls in pursuit of fly balls. It was common knowledge that Reiser played every game with great hustle and *spirit*.

Our God not only *acts* with great spirit, but He *is* spirit! God is not composed of matter, and He does not possess a physical nature. He is not the "Great Dodger in the Sky" or "the man upstairs." It is disrespectful to refer to Him in these terms. Because God is spirit, He is invisible. Because God is spirit, it is inaccurate to picture Him in our minds as an old man with a white beard. Because God is spirit, He is not restricted by the limitations of a human body. In Acts 17:24, Paul says that God does not live in shrines made by human hands. God is not restricted to any location or space. God has access to all of His creation. It is the invisibility of God that caused enemies of early Christianity to call Christians *atheists*.

9

They were called atheists because they proclaimed God to be intangible and unseen.

However, make no mistake about the nature of Jesus Christ. Jesus was God in human flesh. For thirty-three years, God (the Son) became flesh and dwelt among us. Jesus was literally *God in a body!* He showed us what God is like! Men were able to see, touch, and relate to Him! There are many Scriptures concerning both His humanity and His deity. John 1:14 tells us that "the Word (Jesus) became flesh and made His dwelling among us. We have seen His glory, the glory of the One and Only, who came from the Father, full of grace and truth." Jesus said, "Anyone who has seen me has seen the Father" (John 14:9). Hebrews 1:3 says that the Son is the radiance of God's glory and the *exact* representation of His being. Hebrews 2:14–17 elaborates further on the humanity of Jesus Christ. Some would assume that since God is spirit and is invisible, Jesus was not really God. But according to Scripture, He *is* God. Here is one of the mysteries of God: Jesus is fully God and fully man at the same time.

Several passages state that God has hands or feet. Those passages are called anthropomorphisms, or "attempts to express the truth of God through human analogies" (see Psalms 89:13 and Psalms 18:13–15). Also, there are cases where God appeared in physical form, particularly in the Old Testament (Genesis 32:24–32). These are considered *theophanies* or "temporary manifestations of God."

Our wonderful God is a spirit, a being of great magnitude—far greater than we can ever comprehend. To worship God in spirit and in truth means to worship Him with the right attitude based upon right information. May we worship Him in our spirits, as well as with our minds, and may our worship be based upon the truth.

Meditation Time-Out

How do you picture God in your "mind's eye"? How are your perceptions inaccurate? How do these verses help?

1. John 1:18
   - Who has seen God?
   - Who made God known to us?

2. 1 Timothy 1:17
   - What four words in this verse describe our King?

3. 1 Timothy 6:15–16
   - How is God described here?

4. 1 John 4:12
   - Though no one has seen God, what is an indication that He lives in us?
   - What do these verses contribute to our understanding of who God is?

5. Colossians 1:15
   - Who is the image of the invisible God?

6. John 1:14
   - Where is Jesus from?

7. John 8:58
   - How long has Jesus existed?

8. Matthew 1:18–20
   - How was Jesus conceived?

GOD IS PERSONAL

Read Deuteronomy 5:22–33

The Word became flesh and made His dwelling among us. We have seen His glory, the glory of the One and Only, who came from the Father, full of grace and truth.

(John 1:14)

D odger manager Tommy Lasorda has one of the most magnetic personalities of any professional manager. Whether it's joking about his diet (he says the clams keep looking up out of the linguine and declaring that they're stronger than he is!) or his plans for burial (he wants the Dodger's schedule on his tombstone so when people come to see him they'll know what the team is doing!), Lasorda has the ability to communicate and relate to his fellow man. He has a flamboyant personality.

Sometimes we think of God as being very distant and passive, rather than being close and vital. But our God has a dynamic personality, and He relates to us even better than a baseball manager ever could! In fact, *man's* personal qualities merely indicate that we are created in God's image! Personal qualities enable us to relate to a personal God!

13

Our God has all the qualities of personality. He has an audible voice with which to speak (Deuteronomy 4:33–40; 5:4–5, 22–33). Most of the time, however, we (Christians) hear Him speak via the Holy Spirit through the Word of God. We must learn to discern and obey the inner voice of God's Spirit which indwells all believers.

As the Supreme Intellect, God thinks profound and beautiful thoughts. He has wisdom, knowledge, and understanding (Proverbs 3:19–20). Creation reveals the intellect of an intelligent God who is behind it all.

God has emotions, though they are not "mixed" emotions, and they contain no human imperfections. God gets angry (Judges 10:7), He grieves (Ephesians 4:30), He is jealous (Deuteronomy 5:8–9), He hates (Psalms 5:5), He has compassion (Psalms 103:13–14), and He expresses joy (Isaiah 62:5).

God has a will which He actively fulfills apart from constraint or obligation. He is purposeful, and He plans ahead (Ephesians 1:11; 3:11). He has both the power and the will to finish anything He begins (Psalms 135:5–9). In athletic terms, He is not a *quitter!*

Jesus Christ, who is God incarnate, perfectly revealed all aspects of God's personality. He is the example of the God who intimately loves His creation (John 3:16). We love Him because He first loved us (1 John 4:19). Therefore, we can cry *abba* (Daddy) as an expression of our love and dependence (Romans 8:15; Galatians 4:6).

Do you know Him personally? Is He more to you than a powerful Being somewhere out in space? When we realize how much He loves us and desires fellowship with us, we'll want to know Him intimately.

As a son becomes like His father, so we become like the God we worship. Just as a manager with a vibrant personality is great to be around, so is God great to encounter as we learn about the richest personality in the universe.

Meditation Time-Out

1. How do you know God? (Check one or more)

   • As a loving personality

   • As a personal Savior

   • As a detached Being somewhere in space

   • As a mean old man

2. How do we know that we know God? (See 1 John 4:7–8)

3. When was the last time God spoke to you?

   • What did God say?

4. Look up the verses and answer the following questions:

   • Ephesians 4:30 — What do you think grieves God?

   • Ephesians 1:11; 3:11 — What has God planned ahead of time?

   • Deuteronomy 5:8–9 — What affection in your life do you think makes God jealous?

   • Isaiah 62:5 — How does God rejoice over you?

GOD IS A TRINITY

Read John 1:1–18

Therefore go and make disciples of all nations, baptizing them in the name of the Father and of the Son and of the Holy Spirit.

(Matthew 28:19)

Sometimes even historical truth is hard to comprehend. For example, on May 22, 1963, the great Mickey Mantle hit a home run in Yankee Stadium against the A's Bill Fischer. The ball hit the facade in right field just six feet below the roof, coming closer to going out of the stadium than any fair ball in history! Mantle himself said he never hit a ball harder. Using geometric measurement, it was estimated that the ball would have traveled 620 feet had it not hit the facade!

Sometimes truth about God is even more difficult to comprehend. One of the most difficult truths is the concept of the Trinity. To say that God is "Three-in-One" and to say that God the *Father,* God the *Son,* and God the *Holy Spirit* are all equal and yet distinct in function is very puzzling. Yet, it is the truth! None of the religions of the world portray God as a "Three-in-One," with all beings co-equal and co-eternal. This doctrine was one of the first to be settled upon in the early church, and it became a standard by which orthodoxy was measured. A correct view of the Trinity is essential to our Christian faith and to a true understanding of God. Therefore, we must diligently study this doctrine. Remember, God is infinite and some of His ways are incomprehensible to our finite minds.

In the Old Testament, we see two major thoughts concerning the Trinity. The first is that God is one, and the second is that God is a plurality. The name *Elohim*, which God designated for Himself in Genesis 1:1, is plural and suggests a plurality of beings. While we cannot build a doctrine on one name, the entire Old Testament supports this truth. God says in Genesis 1:26, "Let *us* make man in *our* image" (emphasis added). In Isaiah 6:8, God says to Isaiah, "Who will go for us?" In the second psalm, a distinction is made between *Yahweh* and His Messiah. In Psalm 22 is found a prophecy of Christ, the Son, saying, "My God, my God." The names *Yahweh* and *Elohim* are used interchangeably for the Father, Son (Psalms 68:18; 2:7), and Spirit (Isaiah 11:2; 61:1).

While God is a plurality, Scripture also teaches that God is one. Deuteronomy 6:4 says, "Hear, O Israel: The Lord our God is one Lord." In Exodus 20:3, God commanded Israel to have "no other gods before Him." The Old Testament presents a God who is One, yet Three-in-One!

The New Testament accounts of the Trinity are clearer. In many passages, all three members of the Trinity are in action at one time. Jesus said that we were to baptize in the name of the Father, Son, and Holy Spirit (Matthew 28:19–20). The works of the Trinity are seen together in Christ's baptism (Matthew 3:13–17), Christ's resurrection (Luke 24), the resurrection of all mankind, the creation (Colossians 1:16–18; John 1:1–3), and in the inspiration of Scripture (2 Peter 1:20–21).

Not only do all three members of the Trinity work together, but each member Himself claims to be God. First, God the Father is God (John 6:27) and is Father over all creation. For example, 1 Corinthians 8:6 says, "Yet for us there is but one God, the Father, from whom all things came and for whom we live." Second, Jesus is God and has always existed as the Son. In John 8:58, Jesus told the Pharisees, "Before Abraham was born, I am." In John 1:1–4, 14, Christ was not only with God but was God and ever will be God. Jesus said that He came down from heaven (John 6:33), and Paul said that Jesus found it not robbery to be equal with God (Philippians 2:6). Jesus was given the name *Immanuel* which means "God with us" (Matthew 1:23). Colossians 2:9 says, "All the fullness of deity dwells in Him" (Christ). Jesus Himself claimed to possess only what God could possess. The angels of God were at His disposal, and He knew their activity (Luke 12:8–9; 15:10). Jesus claimed to forgive sins, which only God can do (Mark 2:8–10). Jesus reigns over the world (Colossians 1:15–20) and has power to judge the world (Matthew 25:31; 2 Corinthians 5:10). In Christ are portrayed all the attributes of God. He who does not see God in Christ does not see God at all! Jesus summed up His deity by saying to Philip, "Anyone who has seen me has seen the Father" (John 14:9).

The third part of the Trinity, the Holy Spirit, also has the qualities of God and performs the works of God. He convicts men of sin, righteousness, and judgment (John 16:8). He regenerates life in man (John 3:8). He bestows gifts upon the church (1 Corinthians 12:4–11). In Acts 5:3–4, we see that lying to the Holy Spirit is equivalent to lying to God! The Holy Spirit is grieved by man's sinfulness (Ephesians 4:30). The Spirit's job is to remind us what the Son has said (John 14:26). He bears witness to the Son (John 15:26). He declares what He hears from the Son and brings glory to the Son (John 16:13–14).

In summary, our God is "Three-in-One!" The Father, Son and Holy Spirit are co-equal and co-eternal. The role of each differs, and one may even subordinate Himself to the other as Jesus subordinated Himself to the Father! Yet, none is inferior in *essence!* Our finite minds cannot grasp the mystery of the Infinite, nor can we simplify God. We simply praise and glorify our God!

Just as it is hard to conceive of Mickey Mantle's home run going over 210 yards in the air, so it is difficult, yet vital, to try to understand the triune nature of our God.

Meditation Time-Out

1. Why is a knowledge of the Trinity important? Can you deny the existence and role of any member of the Trinity and still live effectively as a Christian?

2. Belief in the Trinity is one measure of true Christianity. Satan uses cults to continually trip up believers in their walk with Christ. The Jehovah's Witness cult, Mormonism, and others deny this basic doctrine. How can you help a friend who is trapped in these groups?

3. What do these verses confirm regarding the Trinity?
    *   John 1:33–34
    *   John 14:16, 26
    *   John 16:13–15
    *   John 20:21–22
    *   Acts 2:33, 38
    *   1 Corinthians 12:4–6
    *   Galatians 4:6
    *   Romans 15:16
    *   2 Corinthians 1:21–22
    *   Ephesians 1:3–14

4. Meditate upon this statement: "Try to explain the Trinity, and you'll lose your mind; but try to deny it, and you'll lose your soul!"

GOD IS INFINITE

Read Isaiah 40:12–31

The Lord is the everlasting God, the Creator of the ends of the earth. He will not grow tired or weary, and His understanding no one can fathom.

(Isaiah 40:28)

What amazing talent John Elway possesses! "He did some things that I have never seen people do," said Scott Marshall, a high school teammate of Elway's. "Once he told me to go to the fifty-yard line and he stood by the goal line. He said, 'Throw the football up in the air and I'll hit it out of the air with this one.' "[1] He did! Elway's talent seemed almost unlimited.

The God of the universe *is* unlimited and unlimitable. He is great and greatly to be praised! There is nothing that God cannot do. No person or thing can limit God. The greatness of God is beyond our comprehension (Psalms 145:3). Romans 11:34 says, "Who has known the mind of the Lord? Or who has been His counselor?" In Exodus 15:11, Moses asks, "Who among the gods is like you?" In Psalms 139:6, the psalmist is pondering the omniscience and omnipresence of the Lord and says, "Such knowledge is too wonderful for me, it is too high,

23

I cannot attain it"(NKJV). All our thoughts, even when stretched beyond their wildest limits, fall short of the greatness of God. Our finite minds cannot comprehend the infinity of God.

Though He has revealed many truths to us, there is a mystery about God. His greatness goes beyond our understanding. Yet, our faith remains weak because we do not see God on a higher level. We view God as being on only a slightly higher level than ourselves. But when we begin to understand the greatness of God, we see things in their proper perspective.

J. I. Packer, in his book *Knowing God*, suggests two steps in forming a correct idea of God's greatness.[2] The first is to remove from our thoughts the limits that would make Him small. In other words, we must consciously remind ourselves of the greatness of God and reject thoughts that make Him less than He is. Practically, we can do this by meditating on Isaiah 40, Psalms 139, or Job 38–41. We must let the greatness of God saturate our souls. The second step is to compare God with powers and forces which we regard as great. The Bible does this in Isaiah 40. Verse 12 implies that God has measured the waters of earth in the hollow of His hand, held the earth's dust in a basket, and weighed the mountains and the hills! In comparison, the nations are like a drop in a bucket against the greatness of God (v. 15)! Wow! The great powers of the world (Russia, China, and the U.S.) are nothing before Him! Our fear of God should greatly exceed our fear of a Communist takeover. All the inhabitants of the earth are like grasshoppers to God (v. 22), and it is God, not man, who is in control (v. 23–24). In verse 25, God says, "To whom will you compare me? Or who is my equal?" Who compares with God? No one! He continues in verse 26, "Lift up your eyes and look to the heavens: Who created all these? He who brings out the starry host one by one and calls them each by name. Because of His great power and mighty strength, not one of them is missing." It is because of His great strength that Isaiah writes

(v. 31), "But those who hope in the Lord will renew their strength, they will soar on wings like eagles, they will run and not grow weary, they will walk and not be faint." God provides great strength for those who hope in Him! He is truly on an exalted level, far above our highest comprehension!

Meditation Time-Out

1. How big is your God?

   - Big enough to handle any problem

   - Not big enough for some of my problems

   - Not sure how big He is

2. Is your perception of God big enough?

3. Do people, nations, or even the heavens seem bigger to you than God?

4. What timeless truths about God can you find in Isaiah 40:22–26?

5. Do you have a problem that seems bigger than God?

   - If so, is it really a big problem when compared to the greatness of God?

   - Compared to the infinite power and wisdom of God, are there really *any* big problems?

6. What does Psalms 62:8 say about our response to an infinite God?

   - Will you do this?

GOD'S INFINITY
IN TIME

Read Psalms 90

Before the mountains were born or you brought forth the earth and the world, from everlasting to everlasting you are God.

(Psalms 90:2)

Hammerin' Hank Aaron was the greatest home run hitter of all time. His 755 "dingers" stand as an all-time major league record. Hank accomplished his feats with cat-like reflexes and keen eyes. But though Aaron enjoyed a great career, he aged and his skills left him. One day, Hank will die and be forgotten by all but the avid baseball fan. Even Henry Aaron couldn't play ball forever!

Though Aaron's career was limited, our God is eternal. He is from everlasting (the vanishing point of time as far back as we can see) to everlasting (the vanishing point in the future as far as we can see). God had no beginning, and He will have no ending! No one brought God into existence. To ask "How old is God?" is to ask a question that cannot be answered. God doesn't grow old, because He lives above time, and He cannot be measured by time! He doesn't have to worry about

27

dying, because He *is* life (John 5:26). God does not grow or develop because He is complete and has always been what He is today. God cannot increase, because He is already perfect. Neither can He decrease or He would cease to be God. God has always been in the perfect state of being.

As far back in time as we can stretch our minds, God existed. As far as we can stretch our minds forward, He will be. It is easy to pronounce the word "eternity," but it is difficult to understand it with finite minds. Stephen Charnock says, "Eternity is contrary to time and is therefore a permanent and immutable (unchanging) state, a perfect possession of life without any variation."[3] A look at Psalms 90:2 (quoted earlier) will help give us a clearer understanding of this concept. Six truths proceed from this verse. First, we see that the world had a beginning. Second, the world exists because God brought it into being and is sustaining it (see Colossians 1:14–18). Third, God was in existence before the world. Fourth, God existed from eternity past. Fifth, God shall exist through eternity future. Sixth, there is but one God, one eternal Being (*"You* are God"). As we meditate upon the eternity of God, we should come to the same conclusion as Job in Job 36:26, "How great is God—beyond our understanding! The number of His years is past finding out!" Praise God!

As athletes grow older, their skills diminish, and they are no longer wanted by pro teams. But our God is infinite in time, and He will not grow older. His skills never change!

Meditation Time-Out

1. How did God the Father identify Himself in Exodus 3:14?

2. How did Jesus the Son identify Himself in John 8:58?

3. Let your mind run backward in time as far as possible. Now let it run forward. Can you comprehend the concept of eternity?

4. When you meditate, think of God as having no beginning and no ending.

5. Psalms 139:13–16 tells us of God's oversight of your development.

   • Did you realize that from the day you were conceived you would live for an eternity?

6. Everyone will spend eternity in one of two places — Heaven or Hell. Where will you spend eternity?

   • 1 John 5:11–12 says, "God has given us eternal life and this life is in His Son. He who has the Son has life; he who does not have the Son of God does not have life." Therefore, to spend eternity with God in Heaven, you must have the Son of God — Jesus Christ — in your heart now!

GOD'S INFINITE KNOWLEDGE

Read Psalms 139:1–6

Before a word is on my tongue you know it completely, O Lord.

(Psalms 139:4)

I n the fencing quarterfinals of the 1936 Olympics, Italian Giancarlo Cornaggia-Medici demonstrated a great knowledge and awareness of distance. Perplexed by two close calls, he insisted his opponent's sword was too long. Exact measurement revealed that, in fact, his opponent's was indeed one-half inch too long!

Though Cornaggia-Medici's perception was keen, our God is *omniscient*. He knows all things at all times. God's knowledge is all inclusive. From the beginning He knows the end, and from the end He knows the beginning. There is nothing God does not know. When we make a decision, we make it with our limited knowledge. We consider the past, or what we know and what we perceive of the past. But our perceptions are often wrong. We consider the present, or what we see before us as we know it. Finally, we consider what we might think will happen in the future. However, no man knows the future! But God always acts with all the facts. He knows the

past, the present, and the future perfectly. There was never a
time in eternity when God didn't know all things!

Man acquires wisdom by experience. God has it by His
very essence. He *is* wisdom! Compare man's thought patterns
with God's thought patterns. When *we* think, we can only
think of one thing at a time. We think a thought and build on
that thought. When we think of something in the past we cannot be thinking of something in the future at the same time.
Try it! It's impossible! We are made to be able to think only
one thought at a time. But God doesn't think like we think.
He knows all things perfectly. He knows the past, present, and
future in the same thought. Because of His omniscience, God
can be trusted when He commands us to do something. God
has developed the wisest plan that could be devised. God has
never had to revise anything or change His mind because He
didn't know the outcome. We change our minds because we
discover new things and gather further information, but God
never has to change His mind and never discovers new things.
He already knows everything! This is called his *foreknowl-
edge*. He knows everything beforehand. He is never surprised
and never caught off guard by anything man or Satan does!

In order to understand these marvelous truths, we must
have help from Scripture. The Bible has much to say about
God's infinite knowledge, for unless God knows all things, we
could not be judged fairly. Unless He is omniscient, His judgment could be questioned. But there will be no debating with
God, because He knows all things. He can rightly judge everyone. The Psalmist says, "You know when I sit and when I
rise; you perceive my thoughts from afar. You discern my
going out and my lying down; you are familiar with all my
ways. Before a word is on my tongue you know it completely,
O Lord" (139:2–4). In Ezekiel 11:5, God says that He knows
what is going through the minds of the Israelites. In Hebrews
4:12, the Bible says that the Word of God is able to judge the

thoughts and attitudes of the heart. This passage assumes that
God knows our thoughts and attitudes. In the very next verse,
it says, "Nothing in all creation is hidden from God's sight.
Everything is uncovered and laid bare before the eyes of Him
to whom we must give account." God *can* and *will* rightly
judge. He is a righteous Judge because He has all the facts.
Not one thing through all eternity has ever escaped God's notice. What a comfort this is to the Christian! He knows us
intimately. He knows all of our trials and allows each to come
into our lives. Psalms 56:8 reveals that God has recorded
every tear we've ever shed! Surely we can trust a God who
knows us so well!

Not only does God know man perfectly, but He also
knows all His created beings perfectly. For example, He
knows about young ravens and their need for food (Job
38:41). He knows how to use a worm to accomplish His purpose (Jonah 4:7). All the birds of the mountains and all the
beasts of the fields are His (Psalms 50:11). God knows all
creatures of nature perfectly, for He created them (Job 38–42).

It's amazing that God knows man, nature, and all other
created things perfectly. But there is someone else that God
knows just as perfectly. He knows Himself! The craze of our
society is to "know oneself." A beer company has a commer-
cial that says, "You know who you are, you know where you
are going." We are told to know ourselves in order to be
happy and successful. But what if a man finally gets to know
himself and finds that he is a failure, a wretched old sinner!
That doesn't make him very happy, does it? The truth is, we
are all failures and sinners before God! Our happiness is not
to be found in *knowing* or *finding* ourselves. Our happiness
comes when we find God. That is the way God designed us.
People without God may look happy, but it is only a temporary and artificial facade. The man who is blessed or "filled
with deep inner joy" is the man who walks with God (Psalm 1).

Only those who walk with God will never be shaken (Psalm 15). In fact, to know *yourself* is impossible! Do you really know what makes you tick? Do you know what you will do in every situation? No man can totally and exactly know himself. The world is taking us on a false quest, and even some Christians are being deceived! The only One who knows Himself completely is God! If God did not know Himself, He would not be perfect. Charnock writes:

> If He did not understand Himself He would be under the greatest ignorance, because He would be ignorant of the most excellent object, Himself. If God does not know Himself, He would not know other things. Unless He knew His power, He could not know how He created things; unless He knew His wisdom, He could not know the beauty of His works; . . . unless He knew His own holiness, He could not know bad is evil; unless He knew His own justice, He would not know how to punish the crimes of His offending creatures.[4]

Because God does know Himself, He perfectly knows all these things.

The omniscience of God amazes us. We agree with the Psalmist, that "Such knowledge is too wonderful for me, too lofty for me to attain" (Psalms 139:6). When Job had questioned God and the Lord answered him, Job humbly admitted, "Surely I spoke of things I did not understand, things too wonderful for me to know" (Job 42:3). We bow in awe of our all-knowing God!

Meditation Time-Out

1. Think of the smartest person you know. Compare that person with what you have just learned about God. How does this comparison make you feel about God?

2. Are you seeking happiness and fulfillment in things of this world or are you seeking fulfillment in knowing God?

3. Study Job 38–41 and list things God knows that we don't know.

4. Meditate on God. While meditating on God, write your thoughts and feelings.

5. Worship the Lord with prayer and praise! He is worthy! List eight reasons why you should praise Him.

6. If God knows all things, should we not trust Him in all our problems and decisions?

GOD'S INFINITY
IN SPACE

Read Psalms 139:7–18

Where can I go from your spirit? Where can I flee from your presence?

(Psalms 139:7)

Middle linebackers must be agile enough to avoid blockers, mobile enough to run down opposing ball carriers, and hostile enough to bring them down when they catch them! Men with names like Bosworth, Taylor, and Singletary make their living running all over the field making tackles. At times, they seem to the opposing quarterback to be almost omnipresent!

While a good linebacker may seem to be omnipresent, God *is* omnipresent. As God cannot be measured in time or knowledge, neither can He be measured in space. He cannot be localized. God has access to all His creation at all times. As the question, "How old is God?" cannot be answered, so the question, "How big is God?" cannot be answered!

Stephen Charnock comments:

As all times are a moment to his eternity, so all places are as a point to his essence. As He was before and beyond all time, so He is above and beyond all place . . . as a moment cannot be conceived from eternity, where in God was not in being, so a space cannot be conceived in the mind of God wherein God is not present. He is not contained in the world nor in the heavens: 1 Kings 8:27 says, 'But will God indeed dwell on the earth? Behold the heaven of heavens cannot contain thee.'[5]

In Jeremiah 23:23–24, God says, " 'Am I only a God nearby,' declares the LORD, 'and not a God far away? Can anyone hide in secret places so that I cannot see him?,' declares the LORD. 'Do not I fill heaven and earth?' " Yes, the presence of God fills the heavens and the earth! God is present everywhere at all times. What an amazing thought! As you earlier let your mind go backward and forward in time as far as it would go, now let your mind travel through space from star to star and from one galaxy to the next and to the most remote part of the universe. God is present there and beyond, and He has all of it in the palm of His hand!

Psalms 139:7–12 gives a vivid picture of what the human mind perceives when contemplating the omnipresence of God. The Psalmist tries to imagine a place where God is not present. His mind runs from the top of heaven to the bottom of the grave and from the wings of the dawn to the most remote part of the sea and concludes, "You are there." Realizing there is no place he can go, his mind turns to the darkness which hides him and comes to the conclusion that the night is as bright as the day to God. If we try to find a hiding place where God is not present, we will only become frustrated.

God is not like a *superman,* flying from point to point. He is already present everywhere! God's omnipresence is quite discomforting to those who want to do evil. It is also an uncomfortable truth for Christians who disobey God, for we get the overwhelming sense of being "caught in the act." In the midst of sin or immediately following, we realize the presence of God. It is when we sin that Proverbs 15:3 comes to life in our experience: "The eyes of the Lord are everywhere, keeping watch on the wicked and the good." Adam's sin of disobedience led to another deception when he tried to hide himself from God (Genesis 3:10). But God knew where Adam was hidden because God was already there! No human eyes beheld Cain killing Abel, but God saw it. David took great pains to cover up his adultery and murder, but God saw it. It was as impossible for them to hide as it is for us.

In contrast to the discomfort that the omnipresence of God brings to sinners is the joy and comfort it brings to those who walk with Him. The presence of God comforts us in many situations. First, His presence is a comfort amid the temptations of life. He is present with us and ready to deliver us. His omnipresence guarantees that He is with us even during Satan's most severe attacks.

Second, the omnipresence of God comforts us in our afflictions. Psalms 46:1 says, "God is our refuge and strength, an ever-present help in trouble." Knowing that God is present and in charge should relieve us from fear. In our greatest despair and need, God is there.

Third, the omnipresence of God comforts us in our worship. He is present to observe our praise and to accept our petitions. God inhabits the praises of His people (Psalms 22:3).

Fourth, the omnipresence of God is a comfort in service. In Exodus 4:12, God told the timid Moses that He would be his mouth. God will empower us for any task that He desires us to accomplish for His glory.

Our God is Sovereign King of His universe, and He is present everywhere simultaneously. He knows everything that happens or that will happen and is a witness to it. God's presence extends beyond our finite comprehension. Our God is truly awesome! Praise Him because He is where He is!

Like a good inside linebacker who seems to be all over the field, our God is present throughout all of His creation!

Meditation Time-Out

1. Is God's omnipresence a comfort or a discomfort to you? (Your answer to this question will help you determine your spiritual condition.)

2. How does knowing God is omnipresent help you trust Him more fully?

3. From what do your fears stem? Insecurity — loneliness — uncertainty of the future?

   - Should not the omnipresence of God relieve these fears?

4. What do these Scriptures indicate concerning God's omnipresence and the implications for your life and service?

   - Job 11:7–8
   - Isaiah 66:1–2
   - Matthew 28:19–20
   - Acts 17:24–28
   - Hebrews 4:13

GOD IS INFINITE
IN POWER

Read 1 Chronicles 29:10–13

Yours, O Lord, is the greatness and the power and the glory and the majesty and the splendor, for everything in heaven and earth is yours.

(1 Chronicles 29:11)

Outstanding athletic feats are constantly remembered and rehashed. The words *amazing, awesome,* and *phenomenal* are constantly used in reference to people like Bo Jackson. "Players from both teams watch when Bo takes batting practice," said one pitcher on his team. "There's always the feeling that you're going to see something you never saw before, and we don't want to miss it." A catcher for the Mariners' says, "Bo and Canseco are the two guys that everyone wants to watch. When they're done, you go into the clubhouse and swap stories about balls they hit. It doesn't matter if we haven't played the Royals for two months, Bo gets talked about. Everyone has to have a topper Bo story."

While Bo Jackson and Jose Canseco are strong (humanly speaking), our God is infinite in power. It is *His* power that ought to be the theme of *everyone's* conversation! Our God is *omnipotent.* He can do all things that are consistent with His nature because He has the power to do all things. God has an infinite number of possibilities and the infinite power to execute each one. Arthur Pink says, "Even that which is displayed of His might in the visible creation is utterly beyond our powers of comprehension, still less are we able to conceive of omnipotence itself. There is infinitely more power lodged in the nature of God than is expressed in all His works."[6] We cannot comprehend His power by His works, for His power is greater than His works. God can do infinitely more than He has done or will do! God has an eternity of power, and throughout the rest of eternity we will see God display His power in ways we have never seen before!

Can God really do *all* things? Yes and no. God can do all things that are consistent with His nature. It is not within the nature of God to sin or to act in an evil way. It is also not within Him to *uncreate* the past. It is true that we are forgiven, but what we did still happened. Even if God created the world and then dissolved it, it would still be true that He created the world. So, to answer the question, we say yes, God can do all things; and no, He cannot do anything against His nature. What a comfort to know we have such a good *and* powerful God!

We must define the omnipotence of God. Charnock writes:

> The power of God is that ability and strength whereby He can bring to pass whatsoever He pleases; whatsoever His infinite wisdom can direct, and whatsoever the infinite purity of His will can resolve . . . As God had an ability to create before He did create, He had power before He acted that power without. Power notes the principle of the action and therefore is greater than the act itself . . . God's power is like Himself: infinite, eternal, incomprehensible; it can neither be checked, restrained, nor frustrated by the creature.[7]

What a marvelous act is the creation of all things out of nothing, but how much greater is the Creator who created! Our God spoke, and the worlds came into existence. Out of *no* existing materials He brought everything that is into being!

It is God's very nature that demands He be omnipotent. God is not some make-believe monarch. He is the King of Kings. None of His purposes can be thwarted (Job 42:2), and all that He desires or promises, He does (Psalms 115:3; Psalms 135:5–6). As it is God's nature to know all things and to see all things, so it is His nature to do all good things. All of God's counsels would be vain if He did not have the power to execute them. If God only had the knowledge of creating the universe and not the power to create it, we would not be here! Millard Erickson reasons that if man is to accomplish anything, he must have the knowledge, the will to perform, and the ability to complete the action.[8] If we fail in any of these areas, the effort is vain. However, God always has all three factors at work! He is wise, so He knows what to do. He is good, so He chooses rightly. He is powerful, so He is able to complete His project! He has the ability to do all He wills to do.

Consider those architects who are capable of building great skyscrapers. They use all the different materials—wood, metal, aluminum, and steel to build a beautiful building. Or consider a young boy who builds a model airplane. He takes all the pieces—sometimes five hundred or more—out of the box and scatters them on the table. Then he takes one piece at a time and builds the airplane. Man is adept at taking materials and making something out of them. But could you imagine building a big skyscraper or a model airplane with no materials with which to build? That's exactly how God created the universe! He created it without any materials. His omniscience designed it, and His omnipotence brought it into being. He created it by commanding that it exist! In Genesis 1, God said,

"Let there be . . . ," and there was. Psalms 33:9 says, "For He spoke, and it came to be; He commanded, and it [earth] stood firm." By the speaking of His mouth — just as we would speak to one another — God created the universe! Does God not have a voice that should be heard? Our problem is that we listen when E. F. Hutton talks and not when God talks! We take God too lightly. What an awesome Being God must be, to bring the universe into existence by simply speaking!

After creating, the Bible says that on the seventh day God rested. But God did not have to rest because He was tired. God is inexhaustible. He *rested* to look back upon His creation and know that it was good. We get tired when we exert ourselves. No matter how much or how little we do during the day, we need sleep at night because we are tired. But God never gets tired or runs out of energy. God had the same energy before He created as He had after He created! His power is inexhaustible. He never becomes weary or tired (Isaiah 40:28).

Not only do we see God's power in creation, but we also see God's power in *controlling* creation. God can suspend the natural laws He established in creation. He appeared to Moses in a burning bush (Exodus 3:1–5); He parted the Red Sea (Exodus 14:21–31); He turned bitter water sweet (Exodus 15:22–27); He produced manna and meat from heaven daily (Exodus 16:1–21). Consider Jesus, who raised Lazarus from the dead (John 11:30–46). Consider Him calming a violent storm and the waves of a sea by saying, "Peace, be still" (Mark 4:35–41). Consider Jesus' resurrection (John 20:1–2), His ascension into heaven, and His return to earth for His people (1 Thessalonians 4:16). There are numerous demonstrations of His power in history. God's power has been evident since the Garden of Eden and will be seen in the future!

God's power is also displayed in the *preservation* of creation. God is the preserver of man and beast (Psalms 36:6). God is said to "sustain all things by His powerful word" (Hebrews 1:3). In Him all things hold together (Colossians 1:17). It is the power of God that has preserved man and the universe, for if God were to speak the word, all things would be wiped out. The earth does not have life in itself. It is *God* who upholds it. All life comes from God. God's power of preservation extends from the ocean waves (Job 38:11) to His control over Satan (Job 1). If God desired, He could wipe Satan out of existence as quickly as He commanded. As it is, God restrains Satan from carrying out all his evil desires.

We must also consider God's power in *judgment*. How seriously God views sin! God told Adam that he would die if he ate from the tree of the knowledge of good and evil. In Genesis 6–9, God flooded the whole earth and killed all living things. In Exodus 19:21, if any Hebrew touched the mountain of God, he would die. God showed His ultimate judgment on sin when Christ was crucified on the cross for our sins. Jesus was beaten and bruised for our transgressions (1 Peter 2:23–24).

Have you thought about how terrible is the agony of hell? As eye has not seen nor ear heard the great things God will do for His people, so has the eye not seen the terrible punishment of hell. The punishment of hell is beyond our imagination. We must take God seriously. We are not dealing with a gray-haired old man with a cigar in His mouth. We are dealing with the infinite, all-powerful God. Pink says, "We may all tremble before such a God. To treat with disrespect One who can crush us more easily than we can a moth is a suicidal policy. To openly defy Him who is clothed with omnipotence, who can rend in pieces or cast into hell any moment He pleases is the very height of insanity. To put it on its lowest ground, it is but the part of wisdom to heed His commands."[9]

Because God is all powerful, He reigns supreme over all the universe. The whole universe is in the palm of God's hand. God is the King of kings and Lord of lords. God has always reigned and ever will reign. Man is completely powerless against his Creator (2 Chronicles 20:6). Psalms 2:9 tells us that when the Gentile leaders unite with apostate Israel to defy *Yahweh* and His Christ, God will sit in the heavens and laugh. How futile to defy God. He reigns supreme. Our God is a completely awesome God filled with power and might!

Meditation Time-Out

1. Take time now to give God His rightful place in your life. Find a hymnal and worship Him by meditating on the words of "How Great Thou Art."

2. What does studying God's power do for your faith in Him?

3. With the entire army of Saul against him, what did David say in Psalms 27:1?

4. What did Paul write in Romans 8:31?

5. What was Israel's mistake in Psalms 50:21 (God spoke the words of this psalm)?

6. According to the Psalms 2, what power do the nations have against our God?

7. According to Nehemiah 9:6, what did God make?

8. What do the following verses reveal about God?

   - Isaiah 40:28

   - Psalms 135:6

   - Psalms 135:7

   - Daniel 4:1–4

   - Daniel 4:34–35

GOD IS IMMUTABLE

Read Numbers 23:19–24

I, the Lord, do not change.
(Malachi 3:6)

How things change with time! In 1911, Ray Harroun won the first Indianapolis 500, using castor oil fuel, mechanics who rode in the car, and sand thrown onto the track to soak up oil spills. The Marmon Wasp's winning speed average was 74.59 mph, slower than today's Speedway rescue vehicles!

Our God is *immutable*. Unlike the Indianapolis 500, He never changes. His nature and character will be the same tomorrow as it was yesterday or today. God has proven Himself faithful and true to His Word. What a comfort it is to trust someone who will not go back on His Word (Psalms 119:89), change His mind (Numbers 23:19), or become less faithful (2 Timothy 2:13)! Because of God's stability and trustworthiness, He is like a rock which remains immovable in a turbulent sea. God remains perpetually the same: He is subject to no change in His being, His attributes, or His determinations. Today, men have concocted a prominent theology called "process theory." The idea of this heresy is that God has not completely matured and that He is still developing. Process theologians have built part of their theology upon a few obscure verses in the King James Bible that say God "repented" (Genesis 6:6, 11; 2 Samuel 24:16; Jonah 3:10). Process theologians have made God out to be less than God. For some reason they have decided to ignore the *many* verses that speak of God's immutability. They say that God is not all-knowing. They build an entire theology upon a few scattered verses. This is a *very* dangerous practice. Every verse in Scripture must be applied in light of the rest of the Bible, and a major doctrine throughout Scripture is that God is immutable. When the KJV says God *repented,* it is using human terms to describe a new phase in God's plan, often after *man* has made a change! For example, God's Word to Nineveh was, "Forty more days and Nineveh will be overturned" (Jonah 3:4). But Nineveh repented, so God spared the city (Jonah 3:10). It was man that changed, not God's plan. God always *wanted* to spare the city. His character remains the same, but when man changes, God deals faithfully with those changes.

Observe the attributes of God that do not change. First, His *existence* does not change. His immutability and His eternity go hand in hand. God's life does not change, because God is eternal. His rule is from everlasting (see Psalms 93:2). Psalms 102:27 says, "But you remain the same, and your years will never end."

Second, God's *character* does not change. Throughout life, our character might change quite often. Our outlook on life may change drastically because of some tragic event. Sometimes a person who has a good outlook on life and a good disposition can change and become a sour person because something happens to change him. Maybe he has been a great athlete but has suffered an injury. Or maybe age has led to declining skills on the field, and he is no longer wanted by the team. But nothing can happen to change God. He is never affected by changes or mishaps. Because His character does not change, He always deals faithfully with us. God never becomes less truthful, less merciful, less just, or less good. Likewise, He never becomes more truthful, more merciful, more just, or more good. The character of God is and always will be exactly what it was in Bible times. When Moses asked God whom he should say had sent him to Israel, God said, "I am who I am" (Exodus 3:14). In other words, "I am who I always was and will be." There is no past or future tense in the character of God. He remains constant. Because He is who He is, His love remains constant and eternal. He told Jeremiah that He loved him with everlasting love (Jeremiah 31:3). 1 John 4:8 says, "God is love." Since God is eternal, then God will eternally be love. The principle is this: Because God is unchangeable (immutable), He will always be who He is. His immutability includes all His attributes, for God will always be omniscient, omnipresent, omnipotent, holy, merciful, and just. He is no more wise today than He was one thousand years ago, because He was all wise and all powerful one thousand years ago! God's character will never change!

Third, God's *truth* does not change. His Word stands forever (1 Peter 1:24–25; Psalms 119:89, 152). At one time or another we have all wanted to take back something we said, because we did not have enough information or we acted foolishly. But God has never taken back His Word. What He has proclaimed remains the same, and He is always faithful to His Word. Jesus Himself said, "The Scripture cannot be broken" (John 10:35). Man may try to change or criticize the Word of God, but His truth will stand forever. When Jesus said, "No man can come to the Father but by me" (John 14:6), He meant just that. People throughout all time have believed they could get to heaven another way (through Mohammad, Buddha, their church affiliation, or their good works). They have tried to alter the Word of God, but it doesn't work. Why? Because God does not change! Unless a person enters heaven through the shed blood of Jesus Christ, he will not enter at all (1 Timothy 2:3–6; John 10:7–10; Acts 4:12).

Fourth, God's *purposes* do not change. His plan will be worked out to perfection. What He does in time, He planned from all eternity. And all that He planned in eternity He carries out in time. Charnock writes, "God's purpose never suffers. One of two things cause a man to change his mind and reverse his plans—want of foresight to anticipate everything, or lack of power to execute those plans. But, as God is both omniscient and omnipotent, there is never any need for Him to revise His decrees."[10] "But the plans of the Lord stand firm forever, the purposes of His heart through all generations" (Psalms 33:11). We read in the New Testament of the unchanging nature of His purpose (Hebrews 6:17). What stability it gives His people, to trust in a God who never changes! No wonder each believer in Jesus has such power to live consistently. We serve a consistent God!

The next Indianapolis 500 will be very different from Ray Harroun's historical first victory run, and it will be interesting to see the changes. In contrast, God never changes! Our joy will be in discovering new truths about Him all of our lives.

Meditation Time-Out

1. How does the immutability of God affect your life?

2. You may feel that you cannot trust anyone because you have been deeply wronged. But you can trust God because He is faithful. What do each of these verses tell you about God and your relationship to Him?

   • Isaiah 54:10

   • John 15:12–16

   • 1 John 1:9

3. If God is faithful to all His promises, let us imitate that faithfulness by our unchanging obedience. What do these verses tell you about how you ought to live?

   • Ephesians 5:1

   • James 1:5

   • 1 Corinthians 15:48

   • Revelation 2:10

4. Meditate upon this truth: An immutable, faithful, morally good God can never change and become an unfaithful, evil God.

GOD IS SOVEREIGN

Read Isaiah 40

*My purpose will stand, and
I will do all that I please.*

(Isaiah 46:10)

L arry Bird has truly been a dominant player in the NBA
for many years. Peter Vecsey paid his tribute to Bird in
Coaching and Training Times: "Any living legend can take
over a game in the last few minutes. Only a Bird can take it
over in the first few minutes."[11]

Our sovereign Lord doesn't just control a basketball game.
He exerts control over His entire universe from beginning to
end! His sovereignty means that He either *causes* or He *allows*
all things to happen that do happen. He is absolutely independent, subject to no one, and influenced by no one. Despite
the suffering, violence, and filth of this world, God remains in
control — whether or not we acknowledge Him. Before time
began, God was in control. He has ruled over all creation ever
since He created heaven and earth. In the days of Noah, when
the wickedness of man was great and every thought and intent
of his heart was only evil continually (Genesis 6:5), people
didn't think God was in control. Finally, His patience with
man expired, and God released His wrath, flooding the earth
and destroying all living things. Only eight people and the animals in the ark survived (Genesis 7:4–9).

The Israelites must have wondered whether God was in control, as they spent four hundred years of bondage in Egypt. Driven day after day by cruel taskmasters, they surely asked, "If there is a God, where is He?" Would they not question the sovereign control of God as their own sons were cast into the Nile (Exodus 1:22)? They probably reasoned that either there is no God, or that God did not have the power to stop the madness. But what happened? The sovereign God who controls every circumstance led Israel out of Egypt with mighty demonstrations of His power! Israel never forgot His deliverance. The entire world was shaken! Nations trembled at the prospect of confronting God's people.

When Jesus' disciples saw the Messiah nailed to a cross, they must have wondered whether God was in control, for they fled the scene. They probably asked themselves whether He really was who He claimed to be. After all, what good is a dead Messiah? But God proved His sovereignty three days later, when He raised Jesus from the dead! Satan was defeated, and atonement was made for sin according to the sovereign plan of God! Our God was in control the entire time!

In considering God's sovereignty, we must realize that all His purposes are redemptive. Everything He does is done to bring glory to Himself and to draw all men to Himself, for God is not willing that any should perish, but that all come to repentance (2 Peter 3:9). Immediately after Adam and Eve sinned, God slew animals to cover their nakedness. A sacrifice was needed. Then, He promised a Savior (Genesis 3:15, 21). Unless man accepts God's sacrifice and gives Him total allegiance, he will not be at peace with himself, his Maker, or his neighbor. Because of our prideful hearts, God sometimes uses a big *jolt* to *wake us up* in important issues in life. We must believe that God is a good God, and that He has devised the wisest plan that could be devised. Even in a world of suffering, we believe that God is faithfully drawing men to Himself, lovingly and firmly discipling His children and justly dealing with everyone. Believe God: He *is* in control.

The question often arises, "Does God choose to save some people and not to save others?" We must balance all truths of Scripture in response to this question. We know His *perfect* will is that all be saved (2 Peter 3:9), and He says that "whosoever will" may be saved (Revelation 22:17). Yet, no one is saved unless God calls them to Himself, and everyone God calls will come to Him (John 6:37, 44)! Is God unfair? Absolutely not, for everything He does is right, and He has perfect authority to do anything He chooses (Romans 9; Isaiah 45:9–12; Jeremiah 18:1–7). As clay in the hand of the potter, we have absolutely no right to question God or any of His ways. It is only for us to trust Him!

Men often ask the question, "If a good God brought all things into existence, from where did evil come?" The answer to this question is, "We don't know!" God has chosen not to tell us at this time. God allowed evil to enter the universe through Satan. The Bible simply says that Satan was blameless from the day he was created *until* wickedness was found in him (Ezekiel 28:15). But God is not responsible for evil — nor is there any evil way found in God. He is a holy and righteous God without sin (Psalms 145:17). He cannot be blamed for evil, because He is total light (1 John 1:5). God is holy, and He cannot look upon sin or be tempted by evil (Habakkuk 1:13; James 1:13–15). Satan is active in this world, and *he* is responsible for *all* evil (1 John 3:8; Revelation 12:9).

Another question sometimes haunts us. We may ask, "Why would a loving God allow such suffering in the world?" Could not God, if He desired, eliminate all evil and suffering? The answer is, "Yes, He could eliminate suffering immediately, but He has chosen not to do so." By faith, we know that a sovereign God is ultimately going to bring about *greater* good for man and greater glory for Himself *through* suffering. We can't comprehend this now, but eternity will reveal the greatness of God's plan and purpose. Actually, the restraining power of God's Spirit minimizes the suffering that we'd experience otherwise. The sinful nature of man and the wickedness of Satan would make this world unbearable if God were to allow both to run their course. The coming Great Tribulation will demonstrate this fact. But God is in control, and evil has not run unrestrained over the world.

The real questions become, "Do we trust a sovereign God through the evil and suffering in this world? Do we recognize He is working out a higher plan and purpose than our physical eyes can see or our minds comprehend?"

Another way to consider the problem of evil is to consider that we know more about our God because of it. How would we know God as a redemptive God if there were no sinners to redeem? How would we know Him as Savior if we didn't need to be saved? How would we know Him as a God of comfort, if we experienced no pain? How would we know Him as a mighty warrior if there were no enemy to defeat? How would we know Him as a God of hope unless we had no hope in every other source? It is God's nature to redeem, to save, to comfort, to love, to pour out wrath on evil, and to give hope. If there were no sin, Satan, or suffering, how could we know Him in these ways? God has given everyone the opportunity to experience victory over these things through the shed blood of Christ. Will you put your trust in Him today?

Larry Bird's greatness in controlling the tempo of a basketball game pales in comparison to the sovereign control of the Lord God Almighty in controlling people and events in His universe!

Meditation Time-Out

1. Do you really believe God is sovereignly in control?

2. We must see God's sovereignty in all things and trust in His goodness and unfailing love. Do you see God's goodness in the circumstances of your life?

3. Examine the following verses in light of God's sovereignty:

   • Romans 8:28 To whom is this verse written? What does this verse reveal about God and His work?

   • Romans 8:29 What is God's ultimate purpose for the believer?

   • Job 42:2 Can God's plans be thwarted?

   • Jeremiah 29:11 What kinds of plans does God have for us?

   • Psalms 46:10 What should be our reaction to the dealings of a sovereign God?

4. Study Isaiah 46. What do you learn of God's sovereignty from this chapter?

   • The sovereignty of God is of great comfort to the Christian. He will place us exactly where He wants us. Rest in His sovereign will today.

GOD IS TRUTH

=======

Read John 14:1–14

Jesus answered, "I am the Way and the Truth and the Life. No one comes to the Father except through me."
(John 14:6)

T exas Christian University head football coach Jim Wacker revealed great integrity during the 1985 season. Wacker was the coach who discovered some boosters had been giving money *under the table* to some of his star players. Instead of turning his head the other way, he dismissed the players. His team went from a conference contender to an "also ran," but there was no question of the integrity of his program.

The kind of integrity Wacker demonstrated is the same kind that God wants to develop in each of His children. Godly integrity is more valuable than winning football games. Divine integrity is based upon God's nature. The word *integrity* means a "quality of being complete, undivided, morally sound." God is complete; He is undivided; He is free from mixture of anything foreign to Himself. All idols are fabricated, but God is the *real thing*. God is all that He claims to be. No man is all he claims to be, and most folks don't even know who they are. But God knows Himself perfectly, and He lives up to His own standard of perfection.

Divine integrity is also based upon the fact that God is perfectly accurate when He describes people, places, and things. Evolutionists say that man evolved, but God says He created man. Muslims say that Muhammed was the final revelation of God. Jesus said *He* is the revelation of God (John 14:9). If God says homosexuality is sin (which He does), then it *is* sin. God is truth. Whatever He says is true, and whatever His Word says is true. His Word is truth, no matter what man may think. Jesus said, "Thy word is truth" (John 17:17), and Paul said, "[God] does not lie" (Titus 1:2). It is impossible for God to lie or to be proved false. Because God knows all things, He is the possessor of all truth (Numbers 23:19). If God is a liar, then we have absolutely no hope. Man would have to make up what is true; therefore, he would know it is only opinion. But God is not a liar, and we can have faith in what He says.

If God is truth and everything He says is true, then everything He says must come true. Whatever promises God makes, He keeps. God proved His faithfulness to Noah, when He sent the flood after 120 years of Noah's prophecy. Most people didn't believe the truth of God's Word, but Noah trusted God, and he built the ark by faith. God proved His faithfulness to Abraham by granting him a son after Sarah was too old to have children. God's word transcends the bounds of nature. God fulfilled Old Testament prophecies of the Messiah when Jesus came to earth. Throughout the gospels, events take place so that Scripture will be fulfilled. Matthew 1:22–23 says, "Now all this took place that what was spoken by the Lord through the prophet [Isaiah—seven hundred years before the time of Christ] might be fulfilled, saying, 'Behold, the virgin shall be with child, and shall bear a son, and they shall call His name Immanuel,' which translated means, 'God with us' " (NAS). He who calls you is faithful! God fulfills His every Word, whether it be a prophecy of the future, a blessing for obedience (Romans 8:28), or a cursing for disobedience (Deuteronomy 28). What a God of integrity we serve!

Jim Wacker is known as a man of integrity. Yet, our awesome Lord Jesus is the only *perfect* example of integrity the world has ever seen.

Meditation Time-Out

1. As Christians, we are to deal with people honestly. Are you an honest person? If there is one thing that causes people to lose their trust in us, it is lying or dealing deceitfully. Let us be people who can be trusted. Observe what God has to say about integrity in Psalm 15.

2. In Christ, all God's promises are yes. He has placed His Spirit in our hearts as a guarantee of what is to come (2 Corinthians 1:18–22). Have you fulfilled your commitments as God fulfills His?

3. The Bible says that the devil is a liar and the father of all lies (John 8:44). When he lies, he speaks his native language. When we lie, we are following the devil's footsteps. How do you feel about telling falsehoods?

   • Are lies okay in some situations?

   • Are lies okay because everybody tells them?

   • Do you hate lying with a passion?

   • Do you feel strongly either way?

GOD IS LOVE

Read 1 John 4:7–21   *God is love.*

                                          (1 John 4:16)

M any people feel that showing love and playing sports cannot mix. They find it hard to believe one can be *hard-nosed* and love others at the same time. They feel this way because they do not have the proper understanding of love. They really do not know how to love in a practical way. In John 13:34–35, Christ said, "A new command I give you: Love one another. As I have loved you, so you must love one another. By this all men will know that you are my disciples, if you love one another." In John 15:9, He said, "As the Father has loved me, so have I loved you. Now remain in my love." Love is not only a command, but it is a way of life on and off the field of competition. A Christian athlete not only *can* love, but he *must* love while participating in athletics.

All love comes from God (1 John 4:7). Because God first loved us, we are able to love (1 John 4:19)! But most of us don't even know what love is! Maybe if we understand what love really is, we will understand more about who God is!

Let us examine a common fallacy about love. Many men identify love as being feminine or associate it with someone like Tiny Tim "tip-toeing through the tulips." Their concept of love is always associated with being passive, weak, or timid.

This idea is entirely wrong. Love is action. Love is committed to excellence. People who really love Jesus will be motivated to excellence. What stirs the heart of the believer to standards of excellence is the thought that all things are possible with Christ. Love is playing the game with intensity to the glory of Jesus Christ. Love is playing honorably with the intent to win if possible. We can praise the Lord for the motivation to perform out of love for Him and for our opponents!

A great number of masculine pro athletes have found real love in Jesus Christ. Walter Payton, the NFL's all-time leading rusher, has stated, "God had a purpose for me in all of it (the events of his life). I can enjoy it and use it for Him."[12] Julius Erving has developed an intimate relationship with Jesus Christ. His love of basketball, though profound, is subordinate to his love of God and to his dedication to people in need. The wife of Mike Schmidt, baseball's premier home run hitter, said this about Mike: "I think his acceptance of Christ has given him an awareness of life that has been missing. He cares about people now."[13] These three testimonies speak very loudly to a skeptical world. Their performances prove that one can play aggressively and show love at the same time.

In the relationships of life, loving is always tough. Jesus Christ spoke with authority when He said, "If you love me you will keep my commandments" (John 14:15). Love involves discipline. Hebrews 12:6 tells us that the Lord disciplines those He loves. Love gets tough when people err from the truth, as Paul demonstrated by rebuking Peter for compromising his beliefs. Love strives to bring out the best in others. Love gives responsibility to others, as Jesus did when He said to Peter, "If you love me, feed my sheep" (John 21:17). Love demands accountability for all the authority it bestows. Coaches or other leaders who *only* show kindness or who *only* yell and scream to motivate will not be leaders for long. A good leader will have a mixture of these qualities. People will follow a leader if they know that what he does is for their own good. Vince Lombardi was known as being hard-nosed, but the players knew that he loved them. Lombardi's love was manifested by teaching players how to achieve beyond what they thought they could achieve.

1 Corinthians 13 could be called "God's check list on love." Joe Greene, the great defensive tackle of the Pittsburgh Steelers, sums up verses 1–3 by saying, "I had one (Superbowl ring) for every finger on one hand and was getting ready to go for one for the thumb. Then I realized that something was missing. It was then that I turned to Christ and asked Him to come into my life and I experienced Him in a new and deeper way."[14] Joe had everything the world had to offer. He had accomplished much, but he was empty. He did not know the love of God. A man can have everything in the world, but if he does not know God's love, he has nothing. Love is the basis of life.

God's love is based upon an intense desire to relate to those whom He has created. His choice to unconditionally love us comes from His very heart! The Lord God told Israel that He did not love them for their size or strength, but because He *chose* to love them. God's love is not based on the lovability of the person. Romans 5:8 reads, "For God demonstrates His own love for us in this: While we were still sinners, Christ died for us." When we were in our most rebellious and sinful state, God sent His Son to earth to die so we could have forgiveness and redemption! He did not love us because we were pretty or handsome or because we appealed to Him physically or intellectually. He loved us while we were at our ugliest and our worst. He chose to love us. He willed to love us. It is this love that God puts into the heart of a believer. Because He loved us, we can love someone who is unlovable.

Verses 4–7 of 1 Corinthians 13 continue the description of what love involves. Let us examine each verse. First, "Love is patient." Love bears up during trials without murmuring. As Jesus hung on the cross, Roman soldiers made a mockery of Him by gambling for His garments. Jesus looked down and said, "Father, forgive them for they know not what they do" (Luke 23:34). It was in the heart of Judas Iscariot to betray Jesus. Yet, Christ washed his feet during the Last Supper. Jesus loved him to the end.

We think that if we could just get rid of someone on our team that things would go a lot more smoothly. We usually would eliminate the one who is hardest to like and who causes the most trouble. But Christ was patient to the point of death. Getting rid of them is not the answer. Being patient and using Biblical principles to reach out to them is pleasing to God. Jesus said that even sinners love sinners. In other words, it is easy to love your own kind, but the real test is to be able to love your enemy. This concept can do wonders for team unity!

"Love is kind." Love has a disposition to do good. It means looking for the good in others and desiring ways of being good to others. It is saying something good about the person with whom you are battling for a place on the team. It is offering to spend time in helping a teammate improve his skills. There are many ways for kindness to be expressed.

"Love is not envious." It does not begrudge another's good fortune. Envy has split more friendships than any other sin. Envy devises ways to bring one down from his lofty position. Envy destroys teams and relationships. Envy says, "I want to be the only one at the top." Envy cringes when someone in our own field is being praised. Genesis 37 records the story of Joseph and his brothers. How envious were Joseph's brothers! Because of their envy, they plotted to kill him. Are you envious of someone? If so, pray that God would change your heart. There is no room for envy in the kingdom of God. Every man is responsible for what he is given and will be judged by that standard and not by how he compares with others.

"Love is not conceited or boastful." There is nothing worse than an athlete who is stuck on himself or herself. A prideful heart does not please God. Proverbs 18:12 says, "Before his downfall, a man's heart is proud, but humility comes before honor." No one wants to hear a person talk about himself all the time. Self-centeredness is not the basis for friendships or for team unity. The opposite of pride is humility. Humility is saying *thank you* for a compliment, while giving the glory to God. It is realizing that talent, knowledge, and opportunity have been given by God. 1 Corinthians 4:7 says, "What do you have that you did not receive? And if you did receive it, why do you boast as though you did not?" The next time your pride gets inflated, remember who created you!

"Love is not arrogant." Love does not walk around with its nose stuck in the air. Galatians 6:3 says, "If anyone thinks he is something when he is nothing, he deceives himself." Arrogance comes when one compares himself with others instead of with his own potential. If we evaluate ourselves as God sees us, we will not have a problem with arrogance. Augustine once said, "Be always displeased with what you are if you desire to attain what you are not; for when you have pleased yourself, there you abide . . . . Always add, always walk, always proceed, neither stand still, nor go back, nor deviate."[15] If that is our perspective, we will keep ourselves from being prideful and we will be committed to excellence.

"Love does not behave improperly." It is courteous. Love respects the intentions of others. It gives others the right-of-way. It means sharing what we have with teammates.

"Love is not selfish." Canter said, "The manner of giving shows the character of the giver more than the gift itself."[16]

People love to be with and participate with someone who is generous. When we are selfish, we show a lack of concern for others. As Christians, we are to love our neighbor as ourselves.

"Love is not easily angered." It is even-tempered and tolerant. Many athletes have blown both their cool and the game at the same time. In order to compete, one needs a clear mind and an even temperament. An opposing team will attack the person who easily loses his composure, for when that happens, the athlete does not think rationally. Proverbs 14:29 says, "A patient man has great understanding, but a quick-tempered man displays folly."

"Love does not keep a record of wrongs." It does not bring up the past mistakes of others. For many years, Jackie Smith was a great receiver with the St. Louis Cardinals. Then he was traded to Dallas. Unfortunately, Jackie Smith is remembered for a pass he dropped in the end zone during a Superbowl against the Pittsburgh Steelers. A person will never be able to function properly if people keep reminding him of his past mistakes. We are always to edify and encourage. Remember, we have *all* made mistakes.

"Love does not delight in evil but rejoices with the truth." Love does not rejoice when someone stumbles or falls, but it rejoices in the success of others. Romans 12:15–16 tells us, "Rejoice with those who rejoice; mourn with those who mourn. Live in harmony with one another." Have you ever found it hard to rejoice in the success of others? There is something inside us that desires all the attention. If we are walking in love, we will rejoice when others succeed in legitimate endeavors. Certainly, God's love does *not* rejoice when someone succeeds via evil means. For example, we cannot rejoice when athletes make money promoting alcohol. Real love does not lead people down the wrong track! But love does rejoice when others succeed in righteous endeavors and just causes.

"Love bears all things." Love "puts up with" or it "covers over with silence." Jesus could take the offense of others, because He knew their offense against Him was coming from a sinful heart. We will never win others to Jesus if we retaliate or seek revenge. God says, "Revenge is mine." The Apostle Paul said in Romans 12:14, "Bless those who persecute you; bless and do not curse." It is here that the "rubber meets the road" in the life of a Christian athlete.

Our goal is to share Christ with others. Athletics is a means of accomplishing that goal. When games become more important than sharing Christ, we need to re-evaluate our priorities. If you slide into second base and the second baseman *intentionally* slaps the glove in your face while making the tag, what do you do? First, you must realize he did this with a heart that is not right with God. If his heart were right with God, he would not have slapped your face. Secondly, you must remember your mission in life. If the person who slapped you is an unbeliever in Jesus, your reaction of love may be the reflection of Christ that results in his conversion. If the person who slapped you is a Christian, you must help restore him to a right relationship with God. Galatians 6:1 says, "Brothers, if someone is caught in a sin, you who are spiritual should restore him gently." You can approach that person after the game in a spirit of gentleness, realizing that the emotion of the game and the competition got the best of that person's temperament. Some people will want you to fight back. They may make snide comments about your so-called *manhood.* That may be the price you pay to live for Christ. Jesus said in Matthew 5:10–11, "Blessed are those who are persecuted because of righteousness, for theirs is the kingdom of heaven. Blessed are you when people insult you, persecute you, and falsely say all kinds of evil against you because of me. Rejoice and be glad, because great is your reward in heaven."

"Love believes all things." It trusts God for all things. Love trusts in God's divine protection and direction. Romans 8:28 says, "And we know that in all things God works for the good of those who love Him, who have been called according to His purpose." Do you believe that this promise means *all* things — even injuries and losses on the scoreboard?

"Love always hopes." To hope means to have "a desire combined with expectation," or "a desire with the belief of possibly attaining." Love has the positive outlook of attaining the goals God wants us to reach. Our God is a God of hope. Psalms 62:5 says, "Find rest, Oh my soul, in God alone; my hope comes from Him." What comforting words! We can rest and hope in a loving God!

"Love always perseveres." Love endures. It stands firm. Love grinds it out to the end. Love stands firm in its convictions. Love endures until it reaches its goal. Love never quits — no matter what the odds.

The last quality of love mentioned in this passage is in verse eight. The Apostle Paul saved the best for last. Here it is: "Love never fails." If we want to be winners, we will walk in love. We will walk in the power of a God who is love.

Even with the tough competition involved in sports, if we really understood how much God loves us, we would walk in a manner that is pleasing to Him.

Meditation Time-Out

1. What is the difference in the way man loves and the way God loves?

2. How can you manifest God's love for others in athletics? In your dating relationships? In school? In your home? In your job?

3. When have you found it necessary to demonstrate "tough love"? How has God honored this effort?

GOD IS MERCIFUL

Read Psalm 103

He does not treat us as our sins deserve or repay us according to our iniquities.

(Psalms 103:10)

I n amateur baseball, there is a rule known as the "mercy rule." This rule terminates a game after a certain number of innings (usually seven) when one team is ahead by a certain number of runs (usually ten). The "mercy rule" has relieved the misery of many inferior teams or of a team that just had a bad day.

Mercy is an attribute of God for which we should be especially thankful. How wonderful that He has not given us what we really deserve! We all have our "bad days." So many times we've "blown it" with God. But He is merciful! His patience is astounding! It's hard to fathom God's mercy as He looks down upon this wicked world. How many chances He has given us! How many times we have failed to obey! When we contemplate the Lord Jesus on the cross and recall the brutalities He suffered, we marvel in awe. What an indictment of our merciless dealings with others! Compassion, tenderheartedness, and pity toward those in need are truly in the heart of God. It is His compassion and pity for us that continues to give us second chances. In Psalms 103:13, the psalmist says,

"As a father has compassion on his children, so the Lord has compassion on those who fear Him." He is truly a merciful God.

Mercy is most naturally expressed in the context of a family or a covenant relationship. It is the natural response of a loving family member to show pity and compassion to another member. Often, parents must extend this compassion to a "know it all" teenager who is going through many changes in growing up. The love of mom and dad provides stability at a crucial time in life. As a father to a rebellious child, God extended mercy to Israel because of a covenant He made with them. From the latter part of Solomon's reign (931 B.C.) to the year 587 B.C., when their temple was destroyed, Israel moved away from God. God reached out to them day and night (Jeremiah 7:13), sending prophets to call them to repentance. But they did not respond. God's mercy toward miserable Israel extended over two hundred years toward the northern kingdom and 350 years toward the southern kingdom, until He finally disciplined both with foreign armies. Then, He called Nehemiah back to rebuild the city defenses. It is God's mercy that gives us hope for a continued relationship with Him.

Because of His mercy, we are still here! We should be so grateful that God is merciful toward His children. Our God promises to complete what He began in us (Philippians 1:6), and by His mercy He shows compassion toward us in our weaknesses. Psalms 103:14 says, "For He knows how we are formed, He remembers that we are dust." God sees us in our lowly estate and extends His mercy. Our hearts should praise the God of mercy, as David did in Psalm 103: "Bless the Lord, O my soul; and all that is within me, bless His holy name. Bless the Lord and forget none of His benefits; who pardons all your iniquities; who heals all your diseases; who redeems your life from the pit; who crowns you with lovingkindness and compassion; who satisfies your years with good things, so that your youth is renewed like the eagle" (NAS). (Note our lowly estate and the compassion of God to redeem, pardon, and heal His people!)

Jesus was the perfect example of compassion in the New Testament. Because they knew of His mercy, the blind appealed for sight (Matthew 9:27), ten leapers pleaded for cleansing, and a man in debt asked to be forgiven (Matthew 18:21–35). A tax collector asked God to be merciful to him because he was a sinner (Luke 18:9–14). Jesus showed mercy to both the physically poor and the spiritually poor. He met the physical needs of the poor in order to meet their greater spiritual needs. Jesus said that feeding the hungry, clothing the naked, being hospitable to strangers, and visiting those in prison (Matthew 25:31–46) was like doing all those things unto Him. In fact He said, to the extent that you did *not* do it to one of the least of these, you did not do it to *me!*

God's mercy extends to those who seek Him and to those who don't seek Him. While it is clear from Scripture that everyone will not be saved, much of God's mercy is unconditional. For example, when God destroyed the Earth with a flood (Genesis 6–9), He vowed to never destroy all flesh again. After a fall rain, He still sends a rainbow in the sky to show the faithfulness of His vow. It's only by His mercy that we are not destroyed totally and completely. Therefore, we must show mercy to those who persecute us, whether they deserve it or not. A person who is merciful would forgive, not retaliate, when someone takes advantage of him. God's mercy is for everyone. He is truly awesome in mercy toward us.

The "mercy rule" can give some dignity back to a defeated team. Similarly, we should be imitators of God and show mercy to those God brings our way, giving dignity to those we meet.

Meditation Time-Out

1. A person who has received mercy should show mercy. All believers have received mercy. God has released us from the debt of sin. Are you merciful to those who have sinned against you? Read Matthew 18:21–35 and make three observations of the servant's attitude.

   • Verse 26

   • Verse 28

   • Verse 30

2. When Jesus looked upon the multitudes, He looked upon them with compassion because they were like sheep without a shepherd (Matthew 9:36).

   • How do you look at the lost multitudes?

   • Do you desire to see them saved or sent to hell?

   • Jesus rebuked the Pharisees because they thought of the Gentiles as dogs deserving of hell. Jesus sat down with sinners. Do you?

GOD IS HOLY

Read Psalm 99

Exalt the LORD our God and worship at His holy mountain, for the LORD our God is holy.

(Psalms 99:9)

A good manager is able to coach players who may have extremely different personality characteristics. Teams need the bold, aggressive play of an extroverted star. But many stars are quiet and withdrawn, and their skills are equally important. The outstanding manager of men will ignore neither. He will blend both together to form a strong, cohesive unit.

If there is one attribute of God that modern man ignores, it is His holiness. Most of man's sermons are based upon God's love. Though God is love, it is equally true that God is holy. These two attributes do not rival each other, but they blend perfectly together. Nowhere do we see this blend more clearly than in the crucifixion of our Lord. God's holiness was displayed as He poured out His wrath upon Christ. Likewise, nowhere was His love more perfectly displayed than when the Lord Jesus took the sin of mankind upon Himself. Jesus said, "Greater love has no one than this, that he lay down his life for his friends" (John 15:13). God's love is not *wishy-washy* but is complimented by His perfect holiness. Time and time again, the patriarchs, the prophets, the righteous kings of Israel, the disciples, and the apostles describe God as *holy*. They agree with all the angels of heaven who sing, "Holy, holy, holy is the LORD Almighty; the whole earth is full of His glory" (Isaiah 6:3).

God's holiness has two dimensions. First, He is set apart. The Hebrew word for *holy* is *qadosh,* which means to "be marked off" or "withdrawn from common use." It could also be translated "to be separate." The word *holy* was used for objects or places which were set aside for worship. Even the pagan religions used the word *holy* to describe their objects of worship. *Holy* carries with it the idea of separateness or distinctness from ordinary or common use. It was this attribute of God that Moses, after seeing the great deliverance of God from the hands of the Egyptians, proclaimed, "Who is like you among the gods, O Lord? Who is like you, majestic in holiness, awesome in praises, working wonders?" (Exodus 15:11). As Isaiah compares the nations of the world to God, the Holy One says, "To whom, will you compare me? Or who is my equal?" (Isaiah 40:25). Our God is far above all creation. There is no one like Him in all the universe. No one can give Him counsel. Who told Him how to create the world? No one! No nation can overcome Him, for they are as a "drop in the bucket" to Him. God is holy, and whatever He separates for His use becomes holy. Man must have an attitude of awe and praise for the One who sits atop the universe. Awesome is our God! Psalms 99:3 says, "Let them praise your great and awesome name! He is holy." When God is present, even the ground becomes holy (Exodus 3:5). The place in the tabernacle/temple where God met the priests once a year was called the *Most Holy Place* (Exodus 26:33; 1 Kings 6:16). People, places, and things that are set aside for God's use are called *holy,* for anything God becomes involved in is made holy.

The second dimension of God's holiness involves His imputation of "sainthood" to man! In the New Testament, believers are called *saints*. The word *saint* is the Greek noun *agios*, which comes from the Greek verb *agiazo*, which means "to be set apart as sacred to God; make holy; consecrate." Believers are set apart as sacred to God and are to be used for His purposes! The Apostle Peter describes believers as, "a chosen race, a royal priesthood, a holy nation, a people for God's own possession, that you may proclaim the excellencies of Him who has called you out of darkness into His marvelous light" (1 Peter 2:9 NAS). What a privilege He has conferred upon us!

God's holiness means that He is morally pure and without the spot or stain of sin. In 1 John 1:5, John says, "God is light; in Him there is no darkness at all." Wow! God is absolutely pure! Habakkuk 1:13 says, "Your eyes are too pure to look upon evil; you cannot tolerate wrong."

Because God is perfectly holy, He hates sin (Zechariah 8:17). He can't even be tempted by evil (James 1:13). God is so pure that not even one single thought of evil or sin can ever enter His mind. Because He is perfectly holy, it is impossible for Him to sin. That's the way He desires us to live — free of sin. What a comfort to know the God who is holiness personified! What a privilege to live for Him!

Meditation Time-Out

1. What does 1 Peter 1:13–16 tell us about the proper response to the holiness of God?

2. Romans 12:1–2 tells us how we are to live holy lives. Study the action words in these two verses. What action should you take?

- In view of God's command, how does the way you
  compete in athletics differ from the world's way of
  competing?

3. Read the resolve of David in Psalm 101. Living a life
   pleasing to God involves saying *yes* to His commands
   and saying *no* to false ways.

   - List things to which God wants you to say *yes*.

   - Now list things to which God wants you to say *no*.

4. What motivates you? Meditate upon the holiness of
   God. As you do so, praise will flow from your lips and
   a deep desire to please Him will follow.

GOD IS RIGHTEOUS

Read Psalm 111

Glorious and majestic are his deeds, and His right-eousness endures forever.

(Psalms 111:3)

O zzie Smith is one of the best defensive shortstops of all time. In 1987, Ozzie won his eighth consecutive Golden Glove award, started his fifth All-Star Game in a row, and led National League shortstops in fielding for the sixth time in seven years. Ozzie is so good, he is almost perfect defensively.

As good as Ozzie Smith is, his skills are still short of perfection. But are the deeds and decisions of anyone 100 percent perfect? Are all of God's dealings with man correct? Whose standards judge what is right or wrong? Is *everything* done by God right and just because He has said it is right and just? Could murder be right, if God declared it to be so?

The basis for the answers to these questions is in the goodness of God. God is so inherently good that allowing murder to be right would be contrary to His nature. Therefore, murder would never be right, and God would never declare it to be so. It is in the very nature of God to only do what is right. The Ten Commandments (Exodus 20) are not just some rules God gave to frustrate mankind, but they are an expression of His nature.

God's righteousness is an application of His holiness. God's righteousness is the administering or enforcement of His holiness. God acts upon His holiness, and, therefore, He is righteous. To describe righteousness, we could say that God is absolutely right in everything He does because it is His very nature to be right, and it is impossible for God's actions to oppose His nature.

How is God's righteousness expressed in our world? Where do we see it? First, we see it in His law. The law of God is as perfect as He is. Psalms 19:7–9 says, "The law of the LORD is perfect, reviving the soul. The statutes of the LORD are trustworthy, making wise the simple. The precepts of the LORD are right, giving joy to the heart. The commands of the LORD are radiant, giving light to the eyes. The fear of the LORD is pure, enduring forever. The ordinances of the LORD are sure and altogether righteous." The law of the Lord is an expression of His very nature. It is as perfect as He is. God's Word is the standard for life, for by it we will be judged.

We seem to have a problem in our country trying to decide what is right. The absolutes of God's Word, upon which much of our Constitution is based, are being challenged. Truth has become whatever the individual decides it should be. Everything has become relative. Rules are being ignored. What would happen if the NFL decided to play football without any rules or standards by which to measure the game, and the players could individually make up their own rules? What if no absolute rules could be enforced? One player may be penalized for an infraction, but another player may get no penalty for the same deed. Someone could say that he scored a touchdown when he crossed the goal line, but another could say he didn't. There would be mass confusion on the field, just as there is mass confusion in our society as we debate what is right. The individual's choice has more authority than an absolute standard of rightness. That's why women can now choose to freely kill their unborn babies. If the standard for rightness is the individual's choice, then what if someone decides that murder or rape is right? Who is to say what is wrong? That is where America is headed!

Israel was headed in the same direction back in 700 B.C., and the cry of the prophets was for the nation to turn back to God. Isaiah 1:4 says, "Alas, sinful nation, people weighed down with iniquity, offspring of evildoers, sons who act corruptly! They have abandoned the Lord, they have despised the Holy One of Israel, they have turned away from Him" (NAS). To abandon the Lord is to abandon His Word and His standard for life. Israel also placed individual choice over God's standard. Isaiah prophesied, "Woe to those who call evil good, and good evil; who substitute darkness for light and light for darkness; who substitute bitter for sweet and sweet for bitter . . . (woe to those) who justify the wicked for a bribe and take away the rights of the ones who are in the right" (Isaiah 5:20, 23 NAS). Sound familiar? We have forsaken the truth of God for a lie. The humanists (those who place man above all) have written a document of their beliefs. Their section on ethics states, "We affirm that moral values derive their source from human experience. Ethics is autonomous and situational, needing *no theological* or ideological sanction. Ethics stem from human need and interest."[17] Concerning religion, they state: "We believe, that traditional dogmatic or authoritarian religions that place revelation, God, ritual, or creed above human needs and experience do a disservice to the human species."[18] What an ungodly lie! No wonder we are declining as a nation of power and influence. God will surely judge America!

Secondly, we see God's righteousness expressed in His actions. Millard J. Erickson says, "Because God is righteous, measuring up to the standard of His law, we can trust Him. He is honest in His dealings. We need not be afraid to enter into a

relationship with Him."[19] Jesus, the perfect revelation of God,
conformed perfectly to God's standard. Romans 10:4 says,
"Christ is the end [completion] of the law . . . for righteousness." Only one person throughout all history has lived up to
God's standards. That person is Christ. Therefore, Paul could
say of all other men, "There is no one righteous, not even
one" (Romans 3:10). Righteousness is to be understood as a
matter of living up to the standard set for a relationship. Those
who fulfill the requirements of the relationship in which they
stand are righteous. If a ball player were to do everything a
coach demanded and to fulfill every expectation of the coach,
then that player would be righteous in relation to the coach.
He would have *conformed* perfectly to the coach. But while a
player may perform *some* correct actions exactly as the coach
desired, it would be impossible for the player to act and perform perfectly in *every* situation. The same goes for our relationship with God. There is *no one* who is righteous. None of
us by our own effort can live up to God's perfect standard and
be called *righteous*. A righteous person is someone who
stands in a right relationship with God all the time.

What are we to do? The good news is that a person can be
declared righteous (*given* a right standing before God) on the
basis of faith in Jesus Christ! The work of Christ on the cross
is applied to those who receive Him. In other words, His
righteousness is applied to those who trust Him. We can stand
in a right relationship with God because of what Christ did for
us! Genesis 15:6 says, "Abraham believed the LORD, and He
credited it to him as righteousness." Romans 5:1 says, "Therefore, since we have been justified through faith, we have
peace with God through our Lord Jesus Christ." Romans
1:16–17 says that the righteousness of God is revealed in the
gospel and that the righteous man shall live by faith. In Christ,
our sin is erased and righteousness is imputed. Do you see
now why a salvation via good works is impossible? Salvation

is the gift of God, not of our own works, lest any man should boast (Ephesians 2:8–9). 2 Corinthians 5:21 says, "He [God] made Him [Jesus] who knew no sin to be sin on our behalf, that we might become the righteousness of God in Him" (NAS). Praise to our Lord Jesus Christ for paying the debt we owed and giving all believers a right relationship with God!

Ozzie Smith is a great fielder, with an excellent fielding percentage. But he isn't perfect all the time. By contrast, the Lord Jesus Christ perfectly pleased the Father 100 percent of the time by living a righteous life on earth. Only through trusting Him can we inherit eternal life. Dwelling on the righteousness of God now will help change our actions in the future.

Meditation Time-Out

1. What "gospel" have you heard or believed?

2. Are you hoping to live a good enough life on earth so that God will some day let you into heaven?

3. Are you keeping track of your good and bad deeds, hoping that the good will outweigh the bad? If so, you have a "salvation by good works" belief and will never enter the kingdom of God. Remember, there is none that are righteous. Stop counting deeds and begin trusting the Savior, for the only way to have a right standing with God is to have Christ's righteousness applied to your life. He was your (our) substitute. He lived a *perfect* life and then paid for your sin on the cross! He was raised from the dead on the third day. Righteousness is credited to anyone by faith in Jesus Christ alone. Paul said it best, "for we maintain that a man is justified by faith" (Romans 3:28).

4. Read Psalm 119 and make a list of all the benefits that
    a person has who knows and walks in the Word of
    God. By walking in God's Word, you will demonstrate
    your love for Him. Your daily walk will reflect the
    very nature of your Savior.

GOD IS JUST

Read Psalm 9

The LORD is known by His justice.

(Psalms 9:16)

One of the greatest hindrances to effective coaching is favoritism. Playing favorites will cause a team to lose respect for a coach, and the players will not perform efficiently. But our God does not play favorites. He saves us not because of our good looks, social status, or intelligence, but on the basis of faith. Psalms 9:8 says, "He will judge the world in righteousness; He will govern the peoples with justice." Knowing that God is completely fair in His judgments can be a comfort. Everyone will have to answer for what he has done. No one will escape God's judgment. What now seems unfair will be revealed and judged by God. Each person will receive his due reward.

Because God is just, He *must* punish sin. God enforces what He commands. He holds man responsible for his actions. Scripture is clear that sin has definite consequences. Adam and Eve knew there were consequences to their sin (Genesis 3:1–24). God has always set a standard for man, and there have always been consequences for breaking God's standard. Romans 6:23 says, "the wages [or payment] of sin is death." Sin is serious business to God and is punishable by death. It was the Lord Jesus Christ who paid for our sin on the cross. Hebrews 2:9 says that He "tasted death for everyone." By His death, Jesus paid the debt we owed that we might have life. Throughout history God has punished sin; the flood (Genesis 6–9), the destruction of Sodom and Gommorah (Genesis 19), the Egyptian plagues (Exodus 7–14), Israel's defeat at Ai (Joshua 7), David's suffering because of Bathsheba (2 Samuel 12), the destruction of Israel (Jeremiah 52; Lamentations 4), and the deaths of Ananias and Sapphira (Acts 5:1–16) are examples of God's just punishment for sin. During the tribulation, God's wrath will be poured out upon evil, and men will cry out for rocks to fall upon them (Revelation 6:12–17). Eventually, God will cast Satan and all non-believers into the lake of fire for eternity (Revelation 20:11–15). Yes, the Lord sits in judgment over the earth (Psalms 9:4, 7–10). He is the One to whom man must answer.

On the positive side, God is a rewarder of those who diligently seek Him (Hebrews 11:6). God judges the wicked and lifts up the humble (Psalm 75). What a blessing it is to follow Christ! Nothing we do in the name of Christ will go unrewarded by God. Psalms 37:17–18 says, "The LORD upholds the righteous. The days of the blameless are known to the LORD, and their inheritance will endure forever." God promised not only to sustain all those who truly trust Him, but also to give them an inheritance that will never fade away (1 Peter 1:3–5). The blessing we receive from following God is beyond our comprehension. If our reward is not realized in the present, it will be in the future. In 1 Corinthians 2:9, Paul says, "No eye has seen, no ear has heard, no mind has conceived what God has prepared for those who love Him." Wow! Incomprehensible blessing awaits everyone who loves Him! That's why Scripture tells us to not be weary in well-doing. Our reward awaits us!

Making good judgments in this world is sometimes a hit-and-miss proposition. Often we fail. In baseball, a hitter is constantly trying to guess what the pitcher will throw next. In football, a defensive coach tries to predict where the offense will run next. Basketball coaches continually try to outmaneuver each other. Sometimes they are right, and sometimes they are wrong. We fail because we seldom have all the facts. We have no idea what the other person is thinking. We're looking for a fast ball, and the pitcher throws a curve ball, or we're looking for a pass and they run! We're expecting it to go to Larry Bird, and they pass the ball to Dennis Johnson! We don't know all the facts, we don't know the future, and sometimes we don't even react properly when we do know! But with God, life is not a guessing game. His judgments are sure, because He knows *all* the facts. God knows everything about us. He knows our thoughts before we think them (Psalms 139:1–6). No one can escape His sight (Psalms 139:7–12). He even judges the thoughts and intentions of our hearts (Hebrews 4:12–13). God's judgment is always perfect, because He knows all the facts. Those who think they are getting away with something may escape our notice, but they will never escape the notice of God. The eyes of the Lord are in every place, watching the evil and the good (Proverbs 15:3). Take comfort, righteous ones, for goodness will be vindicated and evil will be punished!

Meditation Time-Out

1. How does it make you feel to know that God knows all the facts of your life?

2. Read 1 Corinthians 3:10–15. The lives of believers will be judged, not for salvation but for the quality of fruit produced.

- How much of your life is going to be burned up on judgment day?

- How much of your time is spent with eternal values in mind?

- Judgment is a sobering thought. You will be saved, but how much will you have left after the judgment of your faithfulness?

3. Study the following verses. What does each one tell us about the justice of God?

- Psalms 34:21–22

- Psalms 37:12–17

- Psalms 94:1

- Psalms 110:6

GOD IS PATIENT (LONGSUFFERING)

Read Psalm 86

But you, O Lord, are a compassionate and gracious God, slow to anger, abounding in love and faithfulness.

(Psalms 86:15)

Patience is a valuable asset in the sports world. Roger Staubach believes that former Dallas Cowboy coach Tom Landry personifies this attribute. Staubach reportedly once said of Landry: "His self-control is amazing. I know he's been in moods or situations where he wanted to explode. But he wouldn't. His emotions stay inside. Tom controls himself better than any human being I've ever seen."

God is patient. He is slow to anger and abundant in lovingkindness. His love waits patiently for us to turn to Him. As we go our own way in rebellion against God, He waits. He waits out our blunders, mishaps, misunderstandings, wrong intentions, skepticism, and faithlessness. God endures all of our imperfections. Consider the example of Jesus with the twelve bumbling disciples. They lacked faith and understanding. They were fearful. Judas was a betrayer. The Bible says that Jesus loved even Judas to the end (John 13:1). During the Last Supper, Jesus knew he was going to betray Him, but He washed Judas' feet and seated him at a place of honor! That's patience! Jesus was kind and patient with a man who was about to sell Him for thirty pieces of silver. The patient hand of Jesus reached out to Judas all the way to the cross.

The word patience can also be translated longsuffering. The word longsuffering sums up God's attitude toward us. God suffers long when we sin. His heart breaks as we rebel. Yet, He endures. He is committed to completing the work He has begun in us (Philippians 1:5–6). We must give praise and thanksgiving to our longsuffering God, for He endures with us to the end.

Not only is God patient with His children, but He is also patient with a lost, rebellious world. God continues to withhold His judgment of the people and the nations of the world. He still offers salvation, free to all. He delayed the flood for 120 years to give the world more time to repent. God does not desire that any would perish, but that all would come to repentance (2 Peter 3:9). It is God's desire that everyone be saved, and because of this desire, He waits.

Impatience can cause a ballplayer to swing at bad pitches and hurt his team. But God is never impatient. He is longsuffering toward mankind, and He desires that all come to repentance and salvation.

Meditation Time-Out

1. Most of God's servants have had to wait patiently upon God. Are you as patient with God as He is with you? We must wait upon God with hope and confidence, not skepticism and doubt. Read Psalms 40:1–5

to see what waiting with confidence upon God will do for you.

2. Patience is a virtue God is trying to develop in us, both toward Him and toward the people with whom we deal. One way He develops this patience is through trials and testings. Meditate upon Romans 5:3–5 and James 1:2–4.

3. We are to run our Christian race with patient endurance. As we suffer and hurt along the way, we are to keep our eyes upon Jesus, who suffered for us (Hebrews 12:1–3).

4. What do these Scriptures say to you about patience?

- Matthew 27:38–44
- Mark 15:28–32
- 2 Corinthians 6:4
- Colossians 1:11
- Isaiah 40:11
- Numbers 14:18
- Psalms 86:5
- Psalms 37:1
- Proverbs 3:31
- Jeremiah 15:15

GOD IS GRACIOUS

Read Romans 5

But where sin increased, grace increased all the more.

(Romans 5:20)

W hen Michael Chang, a seventeen-year-old Californian, won the 1989 French Open Tennis Tournament, he became the first American winner since Tony Trabert won it thirty-four years ago. In winning, Chang gave a big lift to tennis in the United States. But he did more than lift the sport of tennis. He gracefully lifted the name of the Lord Jesus Christ by giving Him the credit! After miraculously outlasting Ivan Lendl, the world's #1 player, Michael told how he prayed about nagging cramps in his legs: "I prayed, and my cramps went away. Maybe there are more important things to pray for, but everything that happens in my life is because of Him. I get my strength from Him. He's in control. He keeps me going." After the final match, Michael again acknowledged the Lord, despite boos when he mentioned Him. "I know every time I bring Jesus up, everybody nods and gets sick of it," he said. "But it's the truth. He gets all the credit."[20] Michael Chang had received and was living in the wonderful grace of Jesus before, during, and after the French Open.

The Old Testament word for grace is *hen*. *Hen* conveys the idea of "the stronger coming to the help of the weaker who stands in need of help by reason of his circumstances or natural weakness." The stronger acts voluntarily, though he is moved by the weakness or the request of the weaker party. A good example is found in 1 Samuel 1:1–18. Hannah was in need of help from Eli. She was emotionally broken, and her circumstances were beyond her control. She found favor in the eyes of Eli, and he came to her aid. Similarly, it was by God's grace that Noah was saved from destruction in the flood (Genesis 6–9). Also, in Psalm 119, the weak and undeserving David cries out to God, the Enabler. He requests strength to be revived, to establish his footsteps (see verse 133), to sustain him (see verse 116), to uphold him (see verse 117), to teach him (see verses 66, 68), to redeem him (see verse 134), to deliver him (see verse 170), to let his soul live (see verse 175), to strengthen him (see verse 28), to incline his heart to God's testimonies (see verse 36), and to make him walk in the path of God's commandments (see verse 35). By grace, God answered his prayer.

God's grace is also seen in the postponement of punishment. In 2 Kings 13:23, God had compassion upon the nation of Israel and would not let it be destroyed. In fact, if it were not for the grace of God, we'd all be wiped out! Every living creature lives by the grace of God. To Him we owe our very existence.

In the New Testament, the Greek word for grace is *charis*. *Charis* is used 155 times, 100 of those times by Paul in his letters. *Charis* is "God's unmerited favor upon sinful mankind." Romans 3:24 says we are "justified freely by His grace through the redemption that came by Christ Jesus." Paul also says, "For it is by grace you have been saved, through faith — and this not from yourselves, it is the gift of God" (Ephesians 2:8–9). It is God, the strong, who bestows the gift of salvation upon man, the weak and undeserving. If salvation were not by God's grace, then it would have to be by works. The work of man gives glory to man. But the work of God gives glory to God! God's grace is given as a precious gift, for Paul says to the Corinthians, "I always thank God for you, because of His grace given you in Christ Jesus" (1 Corinthians 1:4). The ideas of salvation by God's grace and by man's works are mutually exclusive. These two ideas mix like oil and water. If man could save himself, then Christ died in vain. But because man cannot save himself, the Savior came and died for man!

The Christian life is full of grace from beginning to end. It is by God's grace that we are saved, and it is by God's grace that we live lives pleasing to Him. Many times God has lifted us out of the pit of despair, discouragement, failure, and insecurity. Sometimes we have neither the strength nor the will to endure, but God's grace sets us back on our feet again! In our weakness, He is strong. Grace comes at the point of our total inadequacy and helplessness. Therefore, all the praise goes to Him! When Paul came to the end of himself, God said, "My grace is sufficient for you, for my power is made perfect in weakness" (2 Corinthians 12:9). Paul gladly accepted his weaknesses, knowing that Christ's mighty power was upon him because of them!

When we come to the end of ourselves, we can look up and rejoice, for God's grace enables us to overcome, too! Like Michael Chang, we are truly "more than winners," through Him who loves us and keeps us by His matchless grace!

If God Should Go on Strike

How good it is that God above has never gone on
    strike
Because he was not treated fair in things he
    didn't like.
If only once he'd given up and said, "That's it, I'm

through,"
"I've had enough of thee on earth, so this is what
    I'll do.

"I'll give my orders to the sun, cut off the heat
    supply,
And to the moon give no more light and run the
    oceans dry.
Then just to make things really tough and put the
    pressure on,
Turn off the vital oxygen till every breath is gone."

You know he would be justified, if fairness were
    the game.
For no one has been more abused or met with more
    disdain
Than God, and yet he carries on, supplying you
    and me
With all the favors of his grace, and everything
    for free.

Men say they want a better deal, and so on strike
    they go,
But what a deal we've given God to whom all
    things we owe.
We don't care who we hurt to gain the things
    we like,
But what a mess we'd all be in if God would go on
    strike.

                              (Author unknown)

Unlike some pro athletes, our graceful God *never* goes on strike!

Meditation Time-Out

1. Meditate upon the fact that grace always goes from the stronger to the weaker.

2. What do these verses say about mixing works and grace as a means of salvation?

   • Romans 11:5–6

   • Galatians 2:21

3. Re-read Romans 5. Look for every use of the word *grace* in this chapter.

GOD IS FAITHFUL

Read Psalms 89:1–37

I will declare that your love stands firm forever, that you established your faithfulness in heaven itself.
(Psalms 89:2)

When the great second baseman Jackie Robinson broke the color line in baseball in 1947, he had to endure the boos, thrown objects, and abuse from opposing players and from some of his own teammates. One day in Ebbetts Field, he faced an especially difficult trial. As Jackie was tagging a sliding runner, the player raised his spikes and drove them into his chest. Robinson reacted instantly, and a fight began before umpires could restore order. However, opposing players continued to yell ugly names and fans threw trash at Jackie, howling at him in rage. Suddenly the shortstop, Pee Wee Reese, called time out. He walked over to Robinson as the crowd booed, put his arm around Jackie and faithfully stood beside him in silence. The courageous act of a friend assured Jackie of the support he needed to endure a trying time.

Our God is a faithful friend to His people and faithful to fulfill all His promises (Psalms 145:13). He does not save us from our sin to later forsake us during tough circumstances. When the game of life is "on the line," He is entirely faithful. He will be loyal to us, providing the strength necessary to be victorious! His commitment to us is very deep, unlike the shallow marriage vows many people make today. When He vows to keep us, He always fulfills His vow!

Great is His faithfulness (Lamentations 3:23). It is so vast, it reaches to the skies (Psalms 57:10). Psalms 86:15 tells us that God abounds in *both* love and faithfulness. His faithfulness to us endures *forever* (Psalms 117:2). He is not only faithful today, but He will also be faithful tomorrow, the next day, and the day after (Psalms 100:5; Psalms 119:90).

What does His faithfulness mean to us? It means we can relax, knowing He will be continually present to help us. It means we can appeal to Him for help on the basis of His faithfulness (Psalms 57:3; Psalms 143:1). It means He is faithful to us when we are unfaithful to Him, for He can never disown Himself (2 Timothy 2:13). Yet, He will firmly and lovingly discipline His people, bringing them back to loving Him more than they love the false gods of this world (Psalm 89; Hebrews 12:5–11). When we confess our sin, He is faithful and just to forgive us (1 John 1:9)! What a great promise!

The Lord Jesus is our great example of faithfulness. In Revelation 1:5, He is called the Faithful Witness. He was a witness of what God is like. He promised to never leave or forsake us (Hebrews 13:5). Whether we have just made an error to lose a game or made a great play to win one, He is with us just as closely. Let us rely completely upon Him, and make His faithfulness known to others (Psalms 89:1).

As a good friend is faithful to his fellow player, our God is faithful to us — only even more so!

Meditation Time-Out

1. Skim Psalms 89:1–37 again. Underline every place the word *faithful* or *faithfulness* is used. What do these verses tell you about faithfulness?

2. What does 1 Corinthians 10:13 tell us about temptation and God's faithfulness?

3. Recall three instances when God has shown you His faithfulness.

4. Do you ever doubt God's faithfulness? Does your consistency change His faithful commitment to you? Of course not! Why not relax in His loving faithfulness to see you through every situation?

PART 2

THE GLORY OF GOD

GOD'S GLORY
IS AWESOME

Read 2 Chronicles 7:1–3

When all the Israelites saw the fire coming down and the glory of the LORD above the temple, they knelt on the pavement with their faces to the ground, and they worshipped and gave thanks to the LORD, saying, "He is good, His love endures forever."

(2 Chronicles 7:3)

There has been plenty of glory in baseball's World Series. Who can forget Billy Mazeroski's home run in the bottom of the ninth to give the Pirates an incredible victory over the Yankees in the seventh game of the 1960 Series? How about Reggie Jackson's three home runs in three consecutive at-bats in the sixth game of the 1977 Series? Unforgettable! Or Kirk Gibson in 1988? With the Dodgers trailing by one run with two out in the bottom of the ninth, Gibby limped to the plate, worked the count to three and two, and hit a home run to win the game, 5–4! No true fan can forget Gibson limping around the bases while punching the air with a victorious fist!

Yet, for pure glory, no World Series highlight comes remotely close to our glorious heavenly Father. Our God is truly an awesome God. He reveals Himself to us in ways that are full of glory. No one has yet seen the essence of God, for He is Spirit. But whenever men have seen a *manifestation* of God's being, He has always been glorious to behold. We know Him to be glorious, or "full of splendor, magnificence and radiance." Everything about Him is glorious. All His attributes, His creation, His ways, His kingdom, and His Word are glorious in majesty. Wherever He is, there is glory. When He appeared to Moses on Mt. Sinai, His glory was like a devouring fire (Exodus 24:15–18). His glory filled the tabernacle, surrounding it in cloud and fire (Exodus 40:34–38). When God's glory was revealed to Isaiah, the prophet cried out, "Woe is me. I am ruined" (Isaiah 6:5–7). But then God took away his guilt and cleansed his sin. Ezekiel described God's appearance as like fire, with great brightness and the colors of the rainbow (Exodus 1:26–28). We know that in the heavenly city where the righteous will dwell, there is no need for the sun, because the glory of God provides the light (Revelation 21:10–11, 23). Everything about God is truly glorious!

Yet, God's glory is seen most definitely in the face of Jesus Christ, His only begotten Son! The Lord Jesus was bathed in the glory of God as He prayed upon the mountain (Luke 9:29, 32). Paul writes that God gave us the light of the knowledge of the glory of God in the face of Christ (2 Corinthians 4:6–7). He is the glorious revelation of the living God! He is God in the flesh, given so we can know what God is like! And most amazingly, He is changing us *by* His glory into the likeness *of* His glory! In 2 Corinthians 3:18, Paul says, "And we, who with unveiled faces all reflect the Lord's glory, are being transformed into His likeness with ever-increasing glory, which comes from the Lord, who is the Spirit." How awesome! As the moon reflects the sun, believers reflect the light of His glory! As we gaze upon Him, we actually become like Him, until one day we will be totally like Him, for we will see Him just as He is (1 John 3:2)! Only because of blindness caused by Satan do men turn from the light of God's glory to the lies of the evil one (2 Corinthians 4:4). No matter what circumstance you face, God can use it to transform you into His likeness. As Arthur Blessitt says in his book *Glory,*

> If your business fails — the glory is there.
> Even if friends forsake you — the glory is there.
> When you are all alone,
>   and you feel you are in a vacuum,
>   you are not alone —
>   you are not in a vacuum —
>   the glory is there.
> When the crisis of life
> Almost overwhelms you —
> When the unexpected disappointments
>   seem beyond explanation — the glory is there.
> Beyond reason, circumstances,
> Fear or pain — the glory is there
>   in abundance — the glory is there.
> Oh, Praise Him.

We are changed into the same image, from "glory to glory by the Spirit of the Lord" — that is what it means to be filled with the Spirit! Changed by the Spirit to look like God — to live like Jesus! So when people meet you, they meet Christ living in you![21]

As people watch you perform, do they see you perform with the attitudes of the Lord Jesus?

Meditation Time-Out

1. What do each of the following verses tell us about the glory of God?

- Numbers 14:21
- Habakkuk 2:14
- John 2:11
- Romans 9:22–24
- Ephesians 3:16
- Philippians 4:19
- 1 Peter 4:13–14
- Matthew 25:31
- Colossians 1:27

2. When you succeed in athletics, to whom does the glory belong? Check the following verses as you answer.

- Matthew 6:13
- Philippians 2:11
- Galatians 6:14
- 1 Corinthians 10:31
- Revelation 4:11

3. Can God receive glory when we fail? When we suffer? When we die? Check the following verses.

- John 11:4, 40
- John 17:1–5
- 1 Peter 4:12–16
- 1 Peter 5:10–11

4. What is the proper response to the glory of God (2 Chronicles 7:1–3)?

GOD'S GLORY
IS DECLARED
IN CREATION

Read Psalm 19

The heavens declare the glory of God; the skies proclaim the work of His hands.

(Psalms 19:1)

Although it is a common occurrence to watch replay after replay of the glories of man's athletic feats, we cannot look upon the total essence of God, just as our eyes cannot gaze upon the sun (Exodus 33:20). Yet, the heavens give us a picture of His glory. Day after day and night after night, in all languages around the world, the glory of God is proclaimed in the vastness of the skies. Consider what is known of the universe God created. The sun — our nearest star (93 million miles away) — is only an average-sized star, though it could contain 1 million earths. It puts out 1 million billion horsepower of energy each day. Its thermonuclear center (½ million miles inside) is 25 million degrees Fahrenheit and eleven times as dense as lead. The star Betelgeuse — recently discovered near Orion — is 500 light years away, with a size of twice that of

earth's orbit around the sun. Our Milky Way Galaxy is one
hundred light years across (one light year equals the distance
light travels in one year—a speed of around 186,000 miles per
second) and contains over 130 billion universes stretched in
every direction from earth to distances measured in billions of
light years!

Our glorious God created it all by His Word! It is to Him
that we are accountable. While the creation does not tell us
everything about Him, it tells us that He is a majestic God.
Whenever men respond toward the light given in nature, God
gives more light that man might come to Him.

Meditation Time-Out

1. According to Romans 1:20, how do men know there is
a God?

2. What happens when men reject the light God gives
them (Romans 1:21–32)?

3. Study Colossians 1:16.

    • Who is the Creator?

    • What did He create?

    • Why did He create?

God's Glory Is Declared
in His Name,

ELOHIM,
"UPPERMOST ONE"

Read Genesis 1

*O LORD, Our Lord, how
majestic is your name in
all the earth!*

(Psalms 8:1)

*In the beginning [Elohim]
God created the heaven
and the earth.*

(Genesis 1:1)

C assius Clay was one of the most controversial fighters
who ever lived. In 1964, the egocentric Clay defeated
Sonny Liston for the Heavyweight Championship of the
world. Immediately, he announced himself as a member of the
Black Muslim sect and changed his name to Muhammad Ali.
Clay's new name revealed much about his allegiance to the
Muslims for the rest of his life.

Names have a way of revealing much about character.
They reveal much to us about God. His names reveal a de-
tailed description of His nature. In the Hebrew language,

names were used to teach truth about a person. That's why each name used for God is important. Psalms 9:10 says, "Those who know your name will trust in you." Our faith in God is built and strengthened when we understand the significance of His names.

But how can we know each name in detail? We must understand the Hebrew Scriptures, where God inspired the writers to use various names in reference to Himself. We cannot discern these from our English translations. *Elohim, Yahweh,* and *Adonai* are the primary Old Testament names for God. In our Bibles, *Elohim* is always translated "God." *Yahweh* is translated either "LORD," or "God," or "LORD God." *Adonai* is typically translated "Lord."

Elohim, found 2,570 times in the Hebrew Scriptures (thirty-two times in Genesis 1), is more of a *title* than a name for God. It teaches us that God is the *Uppermost One.* It is first used in Genesis 1:1, indicating that God is the Uppermost One of all creation. Linguists (those who study languages) tell us that *Elohim* is a plural noun. In English, *plural* means "two or more," but in Hebrew, *plural* always means "more than two." Therefore, Genesis 1:1 reveals to us that God is a Trinity (Father, Son, and Holy Spirit), a "Three-in-One" as we studied earlier. So, do we have many gods? No! Man has perverted the doctrine of the Trinity and worshipped false gods. We have one God, who is a Three-in-One! *Elohim* is the powerful God of creation!

Elohim may be a derivative of *El,* which means "mighty, strong, and prominent." The word *El* is translated "God" some 250 times, frequently to indicate the great power of God. In Deuteronomy 10:17, we read, "For the LORD [*Yahweh*] your God [*Elohim*] is God of gods and Lord of lords, the great God, mighty and awesome, who shows no partiality and accepts no bribes." *Elohim* expresses the idea of greatness and glory, omnipotence and sovereignty, and creative and governing power. *Elohim* may also be a derivative of *Alah,* which means "to swear." This describes God as a "covenant-making God who ratifies His covenant by an oath." It was Solomon who prayed, "O Lord, God [*Elohim*] of Israel, there is no God [*Elohim*] like you in heaven above or on earth below — You who keep your covenant of love with your servants who continue wholeheartedly in your way" (1 Kings 8:23). The God who has made covenants with Himself (Psalm 110) and with His people (Genesis 6:18; 9:15–16; 17:19) is a covenant-keeping God. He is our *Elohim!*

Meditation Time-Out

1. What does Genesis 1:1 teach us about God?

2. What covenant has God made with Himself?

3. What covenant has God made with His people (Israel)?

God's Glory Is Declared
in His Name,

EL SHADDAI,
"GOD ALMIGHTY"

Read Genesis 17

When Abram was ninety-nine years old, the LORD appeared to him and said, "I am God Almighty [El Shaddai]; walk before me and be blameless."

(Genesis 17:1)

S everal names for God are compounded with *El (Elohim)* to reveal the character and nature of God. *El Shaddai* is the first. As we have seen, *El* stands for the omnipotence and transcendence of God, especially in His acts of creation (see Psalms 77:14; Psalms 68:35; Nehemiah 9:32; and Deuteronomy 3:24). *Shaddai* is a very interesting word, occurring forty-eight times in the Old Testament and translated "Almighty." It probably comes from the Hebrew word "shad," meaning "breast." It signifies one who nourishes his people, who satisfies their needs, and who supplies their necessities of life. Combined with *El*, we know God to be One who is mighty enough to nourish, satisfy, and supply all of our needs!

117

In Genesis 49:25, it is the Almighty (*Shaddai*) who blesses us. In Genesis 28:3, Isaac asked God Almighty (*El Shaddai*) to bless Jacob and to make him fruitful. In Genesis 35:11, God calls Himself by the name *El Shaddai* and blesses Israel with great promises. Over and over, *El Shaddai* is associated with blessings and promises (Genesis 48:3–4; Exodus 6:2–4).

Athletic success does not nourish or satisfy the deep needs of the human heart. After upsetting Chris Evert Lloyd in a big tournament, Hana Mandlikova was asked how she felt about winning. She responded, "Any big win means that all the suffering, practicing, and traveling are worth it. I feel like I own the world." And how long does that feeling last, she was asked. "About two minutes," was her reply![22]

Our God attracts people, because He *is* able to satisfy human needs on a consistent basis. He nourishes us with mental and emotional support as well as with physical food. In our loneliness and confusion, He never fails us. He provides us daily with bread. An ancient Greek story tells of a baby laid not far from a cliff by a mother who was tending a herd of goats. Unknown to the mother, the infant crawled to the edge of the cliff. Afraid to take a step toward the child for fear he would crawl away and fall to his death, the mother merely uncovered her breast. Attracted to his source of nourishment, the child crawled back to her loving arms!

Sometimes we run from our powerful God. But our tender, nourishing provider attracts us from our dangerous course, and we return to the source of our nourishment. He is all-powerful and He provides for us! The name *El Shaddai* (God Almighty) reveals both of these parts of His character.

Meditation Time-Out

1. What needs do you have that only God can satisfy?

2. How has He satisfied those needs?

3. What did *El Shaddai* ask of Abram when He revealed Himself in Genesis 17:1?

God's Glory Is Declared
in His Name,

EL ELYON,
"MOST HIGH GOD"

Read Genesis 14

Blessed be Abram by God Most High, Creator of heaven and earth. And blessed be God Most High, who delivered your enemies into your hands.

(Genesis 14:19–20)

S imply knowing the dangers of drug use and the ramifications of being arrested are not enough to keep people from drugs. That was the case in the lives of Alvan Adams and three other Phoenix Suns in April of 1987, when they were indicted on drug charges. Adams called the situation "a mess," and general manager Jerry Colangelo was also upset. "I feel hurt, deeply hurt," Colangelo said. "I feel for my kids. We have drug seminars every year. The players are warned. They have all that information, yet some choose to make a wrong decision. It's a blow to the Suns; it's a blow to the NBA."[23]

Not only is knowledge inadequate in and of itself, but there is a danger in knowledge. The more we know, the more

for which we are responsible! Especially is this true in reference to knowledge of God. To know this next name of God
and its significance, but not to appreciate Him, is very dangerous! John Bunyan said that he knew of no doctrine so dangerous as "the truth of God received carnally."[24] Our God is *El
Elyon* — God Most High — Creator of heaven and earth (see
Genesis 14:22). This name was revealed in connection with
the Gentile priest Melchizedek, a little-known leader through
whom God preserved knowledge of Himself among the Gentiles. This King of Salem and priest of God Most High pic-
tures accurately the Lord Jesus Christ, who died to save all
who come to God through Him, regardless of their human an-
cestry (see Hebrews 7). In the three places where the name *El
Elyon* is mentioned in Moses' writings, it was revealed in connection with God's revelation to the Gentiles. Furthermore,
Romans 10:12 says that *"Whoever* shall call upon the name of
the Lord shall be saved"* (emphasis added). God is not only
the God of the Jews, but He is *Most High God* of the whole
world (Acts 17:25; Romans 3:29).

The sin of Satan was to claim equality with the Most
High. He wanted to sit in God's place (Isaiah 14:12–14). The
sin of man is also that of pride. He thinks he is a "little god,"
sovereignly able to run his own life, to make his own decisions independent of God. One of man's classic poems illustrates this lie. The poem *Invictus,* by William Henley, says, "I
am the master of my fate, I am the captain of my soul." That
attitude is sin! Man is claiming to be like the Most High! He
is elevating himself to sit in God's place. When King
Nebuchadnezzar became filled with pride, God took his authority away and drove him from his kingdom (Daniel 4:30–
34). Then, he learned to praise the *Most High.* Verse 34
records his words:

Then I praised the Most High; I honored and glorified Him who lives forever. His dominion is an eternal dominion; His kingdom endures from generation to generation. All the peoples of the earth are regarded as nothing. He does as He pleases with the powers of heaven and the peoples of the earth. No one can hold back his hand or say to him: "What have you done?"

Nebuchadnezzar had a great kingdom, but God was really in charge! And *El Elyon* is in charge of our lives, too! David recognized this fact. He wrote, "I cry out to God *Most High*, to God, who fulfills His purpose for me" (Psalms 57:2 emphasis added). Again, he said, "He who dwells in the shelter of the *Most High* will rest in the shadow of the Almighty" (Psalms 91:1 emphasis added). Finally, David said, "I will give thanks to the LORD because of His righteousness and will sing praise to the name of the LORD *Most High*" (Psalms 7:17 emphasis added).

Let us know the name of *El Elyon*, the Most High God. But beyond knowing, let us *appreciate* Him for who He is so we will give Him praise and worship!

Meditation Time-Out

1   Who is really in charge of your life? With such a powerful God "calling the shots," do you ever need to worry?

2   What ungodly attitude is conveyed by poetry like *Invictus?* How else has your idea of God, the universe, and of yourself been perverted by man's literature?

3.   How does knowledge of God Most High make you more responsible?

God's Glory Is Declared
in His Name,

EL OLAM,
"THE EVERLASTING
GOD"

Read Isaiah 40

*The Lord is the everlasting
God, the Creator of the
ends of the earth. He will
not grow tired or weary,
and His understanding no
one can fathom.*

(Isaiah 40:28)

B aseball's longest game (by innings played) took place on
May 1, 1920. The game was finally called because of
darkness after 26 innings with the score tied, 1–1. Both start-
ing pitchers—Leon Cadore for the Brooklyn Dodgers and Joe
Oeschger for the Boston Braves—were still in the game! They
must have thought the game would last forever!

While no game really lasts forever, we have a God who *is*
everlasting!

The name *El Olam* is a seldom-used, yet very revealing
name given for Him in the Scriptures. Translated *everlasting*

or *eternal* in our English versions, this wonderful name reveals a special secret concerning the nature and purposes of God. As we have seen, *El* indicates the power of God. He is the powerful God of creation. *Olam* means "to cover or to hide a secret for a time." Every place *El Olam* is used in Scripture is either a subtle or a distinct reference to various stages of God's revelation of Himself and His plan for this universe. He is the "Everlasting God of the Ages." His plan and purposes are not worked out instantly but in distinct periods of time throughout history. There is an orderly progression in His redemptive plan for mankind, and it is all under the control of *El Olam*!

In the Old Testament, God was *El Olam* to Moses (Psalms 90:2-3), to Jeremiah (Jeremiah 10:10-13), and to Micah (Micah 5:2). In the New Testament, Paul wrote of the eternal God who progressively made known His plan (Romans 16:25-27). It is important to note that God Himself has not changed. It is man who changes. It is God's wisdom to change His methods of revealing Himself. Likewise, it is not the method of salvation which changes. The shed blood of Christ is the *only* basis of salvation for men of all ages. As men of long ago looked forward to God's provision of salvation, men today look backward to that which Christ provided on the cross two thousand years ago. With the coming of Christ, God revealed Himself in detail, that all men might believe and be saved.

Conditions on this earth were not always as they are now, nor will they always be the same. After the fall of man, God promised that the "seed of the woman" (the Lord Jesus Christ) would one day come to suffer and to "crush the head of the serpent" (Satan). God promised the Savior in Genesis 3:15. But, for a long time, men knew few details of His eternal plan. God selected Abraham and made a covenant to bless all nations through him (Genesis 12:1-3), but until Moses and the Ten Commandments (law), men were led to God via conscience. When God gave the law to Moses on Mt. Sinai, He revealed how far men had strayed from His plan. The law's purpose was to show us how sinful we are, so we would see the need for a savior. The Old Testament sacrifices which God commanded were to picture the ultimate sacrifice Jesus would one day provide when He died on the cross for all men. God revealed that salvation is free to all who trust in Jesus, and He offers eternal life as a free gift to Jew and non-Jew. Paul wrote that God did not make known the mystery of Christ (the mixing of Jew and Gentile into one body called the "church") in past generations (Ephesians 3:2–8). Only after Jesus died and rose again did *El Olam* reveal this part of His plan!

Mankind is no longer in the dark. *El Olam* has revealed himself in an understandable way throughout redemption history. Praise Him! The mystery of Christ is made plain in the Scriptures.

Meditation Time-Out

1. Study Ephesians 3:2–12.

   • What is the mystery of Christ that is now revealed? (See verse 6)

   • In whom was this mystery hidden for ages past? (See verse 9)

   • What was God's intent through the church? (See verse 10)

   • What word describes the length of God's purpose? (See verse 11)

2. Study Romans 16:25–26.

   • How is the mystery of God revealed?

   • Why was the mystery of God revealed?

3. Study 1 Corinthians 2:7–9. If the rulers of this age (Satanic spirits) had understood God's secret wisdom, what would they not have inspired?

4. Study 1 Corinthians 10:11. What does this verse say about the age in which we are living?

5. Study Hebrews 9:26–28.

   • How many times did Christ suffer for sin?

   • When did Christ appear on earth to do away with sin?

   • What will be His purpose when He appears a second time?

God's Glory Is Declared
in His Name,

YAHWEH,
"OUR REDEEMER,
THE SELF-EXISTENT
ONE"

Read Isaiah 43:1–13

Before Me no god was formed, nor will there be one after Me. I, even I, am the LORD, and apart from Me there is no savior.

(Isaiah 43:10–11)

R eserve guard Ron Morse hit a running, off-balance shot that rolled around the rim and dropped in as time ran out in overtime, giving his father's Fort Hays State team an 82–80 victory and the 1985 NAIA National Championship! "It's a thrill for me to see what he did,"[25] stated an obviously proud father/coach Bill Morse after the game. Son Ron had certainly redeemed the game and won the national title for his father and for his team!

The Son of God has made redemption possible for sinful man, to the glory of His Father! The name *Yahweh* reveals much about His redemptive role.

Yahweh, God's personal name, is the most frequently used name of God in the Old Testament (6,823 times). *Yahweh* is the expression of who God is. This name illustrates the fact that the names of God often overlap each other in their meaning. Derived from the Hebrew verb *havah,* which means "being," the name *Yahweh* is also associated with the deliverance of God's people. *Yahweh* is the self-existent One who in Himself possesses permanent life. He is the great *I AM* who stands alone in existence and depends upon no other. *Yahweh* is also associated with His deliverance (redemption) of His people from sin and the consequences of sin. Therefore, the other primary meaning of the name is "our Redeemer." Any time we find the name *GOD* or *LORD* printed in all capital letters in our English translations of God's Word, the original name in Hebrew was written *Yahweh.* This name was so sacred to the Jews that they scrupulously avoided even pronouncing it! Often they would simply refer to it as *The Name.* The death penalty was imposed for blasphemy of *The Name* (Leviticus 24:16). For these reasons, the actual pronunciation of the name God gave Himself has been lost! Today, we aren't exactly sure how to speak that wonderful name!

When the name *Yahweh* is first used in Scripture (Genesis 2 and 3), the name *Elohim* is added, except where the woman and the serpent speak. The adding of *Elohim* acknowledged His power and authority, but left out the fact that He is righteous and must judge sin! Not until after the redemption of Israel from Egypt was the full significance of the name *Yahweh* revealed to them. In Exodus 6:2, God said to Moses, "I am the LORD. I appeared to Abraham, to Isaac, and to Jacob as God Almighty [*El Shaddai*], but by my name the LORD I did not make myself known to them." The Hebrew word for

Lord sounds like and may be derived from the Hebrew word for *I AM*. In verses 6–8, the LORD [Redeemer] promised to use Moses to deliver Israel from slavery in Egypt. It was here that they learned about IIis redeeming character, a lesson they never forgot! In Deuteronomy 6:4, Moses writes, "Hear O Israel: The LORD [*Yahweh*] our God [*Elohim*], the LORD is one." God's covenant people (Israel) were commanded to love the LORD (their Redeemer) their God (*Elohim*, One who had all power and authority) with all their heart, soul, and strength. What a wonderful description of an awesome God! He is a redeemer (*Yahweh*) who is powerful (*Elohim*). How tragic if He were a redeemer who had no power to deliver on His promises! That wouldn't be good news at all. But He does have the power to fulfill all His promises to redeemed mankind! We can fully trust our self-existent Redeemer.

Meditation Time-Out

1. From what has *Yahweh* (our Redeemer) delivered you?

2. With what are God's people to love the LORD their God?

3. Consider what our lives would be like if our Redeemer had no *power* to save and keep us. Or if He had the power but not the *desire* to save and keep us. Praise God that He has *both* the power and the desire!

God's Glory Is Declared
in His Name,

YAHWEH-YIREH, "THE LORD WILL PROVIDE"

Read Genesis 22:1–9

> *So Abraham called that place The LORD Will Provide, and to this day it is said, "On the mountain of the Lord it will be provided."*
>
> (Genesis 22:14)

One of the greatest worries of athletes is how they will survive when their playing days are over. For years, they are provided for quite well by college programs or by pro sports organizations. But, sooner or later (sooner for most) the athlete becomes a "has-been" and is out of school or off the payroll. Who will provide for him now?

Any player (or non-player) who puts his trust in God will have his needs taken care of. The compound names of *Yahweh* we will study are associated with historical incidents and demonstrate the character of *Yahweh* in meeting human needs.

One of the greatest names is *Yahweh-Yireh*, or "The Lord Will Provide." The background of this name is one of the most significant and touching stories in Scripture.

God had promised and given Abraham and Sarah a son (Isaac), even though they were physically too old to have children. God had promised to bless all nations through Abraham (Genesis 12:1–3), and Isaac was to be in the line of blessing (Genesis 21:12). All of Abraham's hopes and plans of a lifetime were bound up in Isaac. Then God told Abraham to go to Mt. Moriah and offer Isaac as a sacrifice to *Yahweh*. What a strange order! Abraham was to kill the son of the promises of God! His heart was as heavy as lead—but he obeyed. He placed the wood on Isaac's back and carried fire and a butcher knife to the place God designated. Obedient Isaac grew worried along the way, but Abraham assured him that "God would provide." Did he know that even if Isaac were killed God would raise him to life? Just before Abraham plunged the knife into his son for the sacrifice, the Angel of the Lord (possibly Jesus Christ Himself!) spoke from heaven. "Do not lay a hand upon the boy," He said. "Do not do anything to him. Now I know that you fear God, because you have not withheld from me your only son" (Genesis 22:12). Looking up, Abraham saw a ram caught in a thicket. He took the ram and offered it as a substitute. Then Abraham named the place *Yahweh-Yireh*, or "The LORD will provide." Many years later, Solomon built a magnificent temple to the Lord on Mt. Moriah (2 Chronicles 3:1). In this temple, the priests continually offered up animal sacrifices to *Yahweh*, who promised to provide for them.

It was now hundreds of years later. The Lamb of God, Jesus Christ, was marched outside the city of Jerusalem carrying a wooden cross. He was crucified there, voluntarily laying down His life for the sins of the world. Nathan Store maintains that the Mt. Moriah of which Abraham spoke (Genesis

22:4) "became the site of Calvary and the scene of that grand and awful sacrifice of God's only begotten and well-beloved Son, who was put under judgment for sin, and became our substitute."[26] True to His Word, the Lord had provided a sacrifice once and for all! Though we don't know how much detail Abraham knew, we know he rejoiced at the thought of seeing the day of Jesus Christ and was glad (John 8:56)!

The picture which Abraham saw in Isaac had been completed in Jesus! The agony of his heart as he prepared his son for sacrifice was minuscule compared to the hurt felt by *Yahweh* in giving His own Son for our sin. How terrible is sin that such a penalty is required! How thankful we are to be provided with such a Savior! What a wonderful heavenly Father we have! His name is *Yahweh-Yireh*, The Lord who provides!

Though we often fall short in both intent and performance, *Yahweh-Yireh* still provides for us.

Meditation Time-Out

1. Study Hebrews 10:4–11.

   • Is it possible for animal blood to take away sin?

   • What did Jesus provide for us?

   • Whose will was it that Jesus die for sin?

   • How many deaths must Jesus die for sin to be paid for?

2. Study Hebrews 11:17–18.

   • What was God doing to Abraham when He commanded him to sacrifice Isaac?

   • What did Abraham reason would happen if he did kill Isaac?

   • Was Isaac a willing or unwilling sacrifice?

- Was Jesus a willing or unwilling sacrifice?

3. Consider this statement: A test is not a test if you know it is only a test. How does this apply to Abraham? How does this apply to you in your trials?

4. If *Yahweh-Yireh* provides such a wonderful sacrifice to cover our sins, can He not be trusted to provide for any other need in our lives?

God's Glory Is Declared
in His Name,

YAHWEH-ROPHE, "THE LORD WHO HEALS"

Read Exodus 15:22–27

He (God) said, "If you listen carefully to the voice of the LORD your God and do what is right in His eyes, if you pay attention to His commands and keep all His decrees, I will not bring on you any of the diseases I brought on the Egyptians, for I am the LORD, who heals you."

(Exodus 15:26)

B ob Wieland lost both legs when he stepped on a Vietcong land mine in 1969. His courageous spirit has inspired millions since then. Bob undertook a four-year "Walk for Hunger" across America on his *hands,* which he completed in 1986. Later, he "ran" the New York Marathon, finishing in four days, two hours, and seventeen minutes. Although 19,412 runners beat him, Bob was not discouraged. "I knew I could handle the marathon," he said in the *Los Angeles Times.* "I'm a born-again Christian and this was a demonstration that faith in the Lord Jesus will always overcome the impossible."[27]

Can Bob Wieland hope for physical healing in this life? Possibly not. It seems that God is using his life more the way he is now! But there is no doubt that God has already healed him emotionally and spiritually. In eternity he will be housed in a body that is *out of this world.* That's because we serve *Yahweh-Rophe* — The God who heals!

The order in which the compound names of *Yahweh* appear is very significant. Progressively, the Lord is revealing Himself to His redeemed people as the God who is capable of meeting every need in life as it arises. The name *Yahweh-Rophe* was given through one of the first experiences of Israel after deliverance from Egyptian slavery. Only three days out of Egypt, Israel's water was gone, and they became thirsty in the arid desert. Upon arriving at a place called *Marah,* they found a well! But when the water of Marah (which means "bitter") proved unfit, they complained against Moses. They failed to realize that God was teaching them a lesson about Himself. The Lord showed Moses a tree which he was to cast into the water to purify it (Exodus 15:25). When Moses did so, the water was made pure! Thus He proved to be *Yahweh-Rophe*: the God who heals.

Rophe appears sixty to seventy times in the Old Testament and always means "to restore," "to heal," "to cure," or "a physician in the physical, moral and/or spiritual sense." God pledged to be the Great Physician to Israel upon condition of their obedience.

Since the Garden of Eden, mankind has been in need of healing. He needs healing from the sin of his heart. Just a touch from the Lord can remove the blight of sin and restore our relationship with God. Man needs emotional healing because of damaged relationships with others. Only the Great Physician can heal us emotionally. Finally, man often needs physical healing. As Nathan Store writes, "The *Yahweh* who heals in the Old Testament is the Jesus who heals in the New."[28] He began His public ministry by declaring, "The Spirit of the Lord is on me, because He has anointed me to preach good news to the poor. He has sent me to proclaim freedom for the prisoners and recovery of sight for the blind, to release the oppressed, to proclaim the year of the Lord's favor" (Luke 4:18–19). Yes, God is still in the *healing business* today!

How sad that mankind has rejected the healing touch of the Great Physician. He doesn't want to harm us, but to heal us of the spiritual sickness of sin and ultimately of the physical and emotional consequences of our rebellion against God. His suffering on Calvary's cross was on our behalf, that we might experience wholeness in our spirit. His great love motivates Him to heal damaged emotions which have been frayed by the ugliness of sin. His healing touch means health to broken bodies, when He can accomplish the greatest good by restoring us physically. We praise Him that He is *Yahweh-Rophe*—the God who heals.

Meditation Time-Out

1. Re-read Exodus 15:26. What four conditions was Israel to fulfill in relation to the LORD?

2. When Israel did these things, what did *Yahweh-Rophe* promise?

3. How did Jesus reveal *Yahweh-Rophe* in the following passages?

   • Luke 8:26–39

   • Luke 8:40–48

   • Luke 8:49–56

   • Luke 13:10–17

4. How has *Yahweh-Rophe* healed you?

   • Spiritually — by restoring my relationship with God?

   • Mentally — by calming my troubled mind?

   • Emotionally — by touching deep hurts inflicted by self or others?

   • Physically — by raising me up from sickness?

God's Glory Is Declared in His Name,

YAHWEH-NISSI, "THE LORD, MY BANNER"

Read Exodus 17:8–15

Moses built an altar and called it "The LORD is my Banner."

(Exodus 17:15)

A nyone who has witnessed the opening ceremonies of the Olympic Games knows they are a sight to behold. The athletes of each nation appear, led by a flag-bearer carrying the banner of their country. It is with great pride that the athletes represent their home country as they march behind that banner!

The Israelites in the days of Moses were proud to represent their nation and their Lord, too. God had just freed them from slavery and provided for their needs in the wilderness. He was proving Himself to be an awesome God. Moved by fear and jealousy of the recently liberated nation, the Amalekites launched a bitter attack against Israel. It was the first war in their young history. As leader of the nation, Moses chose

Joshua to be the general of the "armed forces," an ill-equipped, ill-disciplined, and inexperienced mob at best. Joshua was to lead the counterattack against a well-armed and experienced enemy. As the armies fought, Moses went to a hill overlooking the battle and prayed. He held high his hands, lifting the rod that God had given him to display miracles to Pharaoh in Egypt, to part the Red Sea, and to close the sea on the Egyptian army. During the battle, when his arms became weary and fell, Israel was pushed back. So, Aaron and Hur held his arms high again, and Israel succeeded! What a picture! When it was over, Moses built an altar by which to remember the victory. He named it *Yahweh-Nissi*: The Lord is my Banner.

In ancient times, a banner was not necessarily a flag as we know it today. It was often a pole with a shiny ornament which glistened in the sun. It meant a *standard,* and it stood for God's cause in battle. It was a sign of His overwhelming victory over sin and the enemies of the Lord.

What banner has God given us today? He has given us the cross of our Lord Jesus Christ! The cross is our banner of victory over the world, the flesh, and the devil. It was on the cross that Jesus shed His blood for our redemption! God gave us a great banner of victory, when He sent Jesus to die on that cross.

We cannot win on our own. As Israel only triumphed when Moses raised the banner, so we are saved and walk in victory only in the power of the empty cross. Our confidence is in the power of the risen Christ. *Yahweh-Nissi* Himself has become our banner! "Thanks be to God! He gives us the victory through our Lord Jesus Christ" (1 Corinthians 15:57).

Meditation Time-Out

1. What is the "banner" of America?

2. How would a close friend describe a "banner" for your life?

3. In what ways can you carry the "banner" of Christ:

   - in your workplace?
   - in your home?
   - with your friends?
   - in your community?

God's Glory Is Declared
in His Name,

YAHWEH-M'KADDESH, "THE LORD, WHO MAKES US HOLY"

Read Leviticus 20

> *Keep my decrees and fol-*
> *low them. I am the LORD,*
> *who makes you holy.*
>
> (Leviticus 20:8)

In Cooperstown, New York, is located baseball's Hall of Fame. Those players who have distinguished themselves by their outstanding play are *set apart* by their membership in this very exclusive club. It is a tremendous privilege for a ball player to be elected to the Hall of Fame by a panel of sports authorities.

The order in which God revealed Himself to His people suggests purpose and progression. After revealing Himself in Genesis as the God who provides salvation and in Exodus as the God who heals and becomes our banner, the Lord revealed

Himself in Leviticus as the God who sanctifies, or "sets His
people apart." Indeed, whenever God saves a man, He begins
a process of setting him apart from this world by directing
him in a changed lifestyle. The book of Leviticus describes
how a redeemed people should walk in a way worthy of their
high calling. Six times in Leviticus 20–21 God refers to Himself as *Yahweh-M'Kaddesh,* "the God who makes us holy."
The idea is most closely explained by the words *sanctify* and
hallow. To *sanctify* means "to set apart." Lincoln used the
word *hallow* to describe what the soldiers of the Civil War did
to the ground as their blood was spilled upon the soil of
America. In a greater sense, God *hallows* or *sets apart* all who
trust in the blood of His Son for their salvation.

Yahweh Himself is *set apart* by His goodness. Where man
is sinful, God is sinless. Hannah praised God by declaring,
"There is no one holy like the Lord; there is no one besides
you; there is no Rock like our God" (1 Samuel 2:2). An old
Scottish author writes:

> It [holiness of God] is the balance . . . of all the attributes of
> Deity. Power without holiness would degenerate into cruelty;
> omniscience without holiness would become craft; justice
> without holiness would degenerate into revenge; and good-
> ness without holiness would be passionate and intemperate
> fondness doing mischief rather than accomplishing good.[29]

Store declares, "The holiness of God is the most important
lesson about God in the Old Testament."[30] Even the seraphim,
creatures of immaculate purity, cover their faces when in the
presence of a Holy God (Isaiah 6:2). The name of God is holy
and awesome (Psalms 111:9). His eyes are too pure to ever
look upon evil (Habakkuk 1:13).

It is against the holy glory of God that all men have sinned
(Romans 3:23). But it is God's purpose in redemption to make
us like Him—*holy* in thought, word, attitude, and deed. We
are to serve no other gods but *Yahweh,* for men become like

the god they serve. As we were made holy in position, we are to become holy in practice (Ephesians 5:25–27).

How does He make us holy? By His Word! Jesus prayed on behalf of His disciples, "Sanctify them by the truth; your word is truth" (John 17:17). As we spend time in His Word, He transforms us, making us like Himself! Our bodies become a living sacrifice, holy and acceptable to Him (Romans 12:1). It is He who sets us apart for His glory. Praise the name of *Yahweh-M'Kaddesh*.

Meditation Time-Out

1. As God has made all believers to be holy in their *position* before Him, He desires to change our thoughts, attitudes and actions to conform to His holy nature. What do these verses state about the *position* of all those who are in Christ?

   - 1 Peter 2:9

   - 1 Corinthians 3:16–17

   - Colossians 1:22

2. What do these Scriptures state about the *practice* of believers in Jesus?

   - Ephesians 4:1–3

   - Romans 12:1–2

   - 1 Peter 1:14–16

   - Colossians 3:12–14

3. If you are God's child, He has begun to work in you to transform your life. How has He begun the process of changing your attitudes, desires, and actions? Thank *Yahweh-M'Kaddesh* that He has *set you apart* from the terrible destruction of a wasted life!

God's Glory Is Declared
in His Name,

YAHWEH-SHALOM, "THE LORD IS PEACE"

Read Judges 6:1–24

*So Gideon built an altar to
the LORD there and called
it "The LORD is Peace."*

(Judges 6:24)

B ob Richards, a theology professor from California, was
one of America's great Olympic heroes of the 1950s. In
1952, Richards won the pole vault in Helsinki with a vault of
14'11". He won again in Melbourne in 1956, this time going
14'11½". More importantly, Richards acted as a genuine
peacemaker in 1952. It was the first year that the USSR sent a
team to the Olympics, and many people envisioned the games
as the *front-line* of the Cold War. Richards felt otherwise. He
became a major force in encouraging peace and friendship between athletes of both the USA and the Soviet Union.

In acting as a peacemaker, Richards showed himself to be
a follower of the God who *is* peace. How did the Lord reveal

this part of His nature? Let's return to our study of Jewish history for the answer. It had been over two hundred years since God revealed Himself as *Yahweh-M'Kaddesh,* the "God who sanctifies." The people of Israel had forgotten He was *Yahweh-Yireh,* the "God who provides redemption." They neglected *Yahweh-Rophe,* "the God who heals" and who would have healed them of all their sin and sorrow if they had returned to Him. They turned their backs on *Yahweh-Nissi,* their "banner of victory." They fell into the most hideous practices of their pagan neighbors — worship of idols, of self, and of pleasure. But when they lost their purity, they began to also lose their peace and their prosperity! The enemy they should have defeated now defeated them and drove them into caves of refuge. It was the period of the judges — repeating cycles of sin, repentance, and restoration — as God continually raised up leaders to deliver them. Gideon was such a judge.

For seven years, Israel squirmed under the attacks of the Midianites — roving, warlike raiders who took everything in sight. As Gideon secretly threshed what little wheat he had hidden, the angel of *Yahweh* appeared to him with a promise of deliverance. In Gideon's restless struggle and worry, *Yahweh* Himself (Judges 6:22) appeared to bring peace. By faith, Gideon built an altar as a memorial, naming it *Yahweh-Shalom* in anticipation of peace and victory.

What does *Shalom* and its various shades of meaning imply? It implies a "harmony of relationship based upon the payment of a debt." *Shalom* and its derivatives are translated *peace* some 170 times in Scripture.

Peace depends upon righteousness (Isaiah 32:17). The unrighteous do not know peace (Romans 3:11, 17). In fact, Isaiah 57:20–21 tells us that there is never peace for the wicked. Man must *first* give glory to God, and *then* he will enjoy peace on earth (Luke 2:14). Only when Jesus, the Prince of Peace, comes to rule will there be world peace. Israel should have been enjoying the peace and rest of their prom-ised land. They had been saved (redeemed) from slavery in Egypt. But through disobedience, the peace of God had not been theirs to enjoy. They had peace *with* God because of His covenant promises to their nation, but they did not enjoy the peace *of* God!

Are you enjoying God's peace? We only have peace with God through our Lord Jesus Christ (Romans 5:1). He made peace for us by the blood of His cross (Colossians 1:20). Has disobedience caused His peace to leave you? Then fix your mind upon Him, trusting Him completely. He has thoughts of peace toward you (Jeremiah 29:11). Isaiah 26:3 says, "You [God] will keep in perfect peace him whose mind is steadfast [fixed upon God], because he trusts in you [God]." The more we think of Him and trust in Him, the more of His peace we will experience.

Philippians 4:7 says that God's peace transcends all under-standing. We need not be anxious about *anything* (Philippians 4:6). The amount of peace we experience depends upon our trust and upon our obedience. You can enjoy His peace today. His name, *Yahweh-Shalom,* guarantees it.

Let us be peacemakers like Bob Richards and demonstrate the peace that exists between *Yahweh-Shalom* and His obedi-ent children.

Meditation Time-Out

1. When the angel of the LORD addressed Gideon, He re-ferred to Gideon as someone he *could* be through the power of God (Judges 6:12). How did the angel refer to Gideon?

2. Read Judges 7 and 8. Summarize the events that fol-lowed the visit of the angel.

- What did the land enjoy during Gideon's lifetime?

- How long did the peace last?

- What later robbed the Israelites of peace (8:33–35)?

3. Name three reasons people do not enjoy God's peace today.

4. For what reasons do *you* not enjoy the peace of God?

5. How can you enjoy God's peace (Philippians 4:6–8)?

God's Glory Is Declared
in His Name,

YAHWEH-SABAOTH,
"LORD OF HOSTS"

Read Isaiah 6:1–8

> *Holy, holy, holy is the*
> *LORD Almighty [LORD of*
> *hosts]; the whole earth is*
> *full of His glory.*
>
> (Isaiah 6:3)

T here have been great leaders throughout the history of
the world. They have exercised command over millions
of people. Yet, all of man's leadership is by permission of
those under authority, and the glory of a human conqueror is
temporary. In the movie *Patton,* George C. Scott refers to the
transitory nature of victory after the fury of the battles was
concluded:

> For over a thousand years, Roman conquerors returning
> from the wars enjoyed the honor of the triumph, the tumul-
> tuous parade. In the procession came trumpeters and musi-
> cians and strange animals from the conquered territory with
> carts laden with treasure and captured armaments. The con-
> queror rode in a triumphal chariot with the day's prisoners
> walking in chains before him. Sometimes his children robed

153

in white stood with him in the chariot or rode the trace horses. A slave stood behind the conqueror holding a golden crown and whispering in his ear the warning—that all glory is fleeting.

The name *Yahweh-Sabaoth* is associated with the failure of the Jewish nation to follow the path of their Lord. Translated "LORD Almighty" or "LORD of hosts" in the King James Version, this name reveals the LORD as captain of the armies (*hosts*) of heaven who is mighty to save his disobedient, wayward people and to fulfill His purpose in the world. The glory of our heavenly commander is *not* fleeting! The name was often used by prophets (eighty times by Jeremiah, fifty times by Zechariah) in foretelling God's judgment on His disobedient people. Yet, it was also the name they turned to for comfort and deliverance when Israel was helpless before powerful enemies. Psalms 46:7, 11 (KJV) says, "The LORD of hosts is with us; the God of Jacob is our refuge." It was against *Yahweh-Sabaoth* that Israel sinned in Isaiah 9:13: "But the people have not returned to Him who struck them, nor have they sought the LORD Almighty [LORD of hosts]." Therefore, "By the wrath of the LORD Almighty [LORD of hosts] the land will be scorched and the people will be fuel for the fire" (v. 19).

Yet, it is the same LORD of hosts who protects His people. *Yahweh-Sabaoth* is the commander of heaven's hosts of angels. We are told that the angel of the LORD encamps around those who fear Him, and He delivers them (Psalms 34:7). Angels guard us in all our ways (Psalms 91:11). In one night, just *one* angel from heaven's host killed 185,000 Assyrians who had attacked Israel (2 Kings 19:35)! *Two* angels rescued Lot and his family from Sodom's destruction (Genesis 19). Angels met Jacob as he walked with God (Genesis 32:1). An invisible army of angels defended Israel from the Arameans, covering the hills with horses and chariots of fire around Elisha (2 Kings 6:15–17).

Angels from heaven's armies constantly appear in the New Testament also. They appeared to Joseph (Matthew 1:20), to Mary (Luke 1:26, 30), to Zechariah (Luke 1:13, 19), and to Shepherds (Luke 2). Angels are ministering spirits, sent by God to help those who are saved (Hebrews 1:14)! Angels of heaven ministered to Jesus after His temptation (Matthew 4:11) and in Gethsemane (Luke 22:43). At His grave, an angel rolled away the stone to reveal His resurrection (Matthew 28:2, 6). Jesus could have asked for more than twelve legions of angels (72,000) to annihilate a world which rejected Him (Matthew 26:53). Angels helped Peter in prison (Acts 12:6–10), Philip in the desert (Acts 8:26), Paul in a storm (Acts 27:23), and John on the island of Patmos (Revelation 1:1). The Revelation tells of angels at the "four corners of the earth" (Revelation 7:1) and of angels blowing trumpets to alert of judgment (Revelation 8). Angels are constantly carrying out the purpose of their captain, the LORD of hosts, in this world.

The LORD God Almighty is a Great Leader. He commands a vast army for His glory and our good. His is the army of the Living God, the LORD of Hosts. How thankful we should be to serve such a wonderful Commander-in-chief!

Meditation Time-Out

1. Have you ever seen an angel?

2. How do you know angels exist?

3. What do you suppose an angel looks like?

4. What do these verses tell us about angels?

   • Their appearance (Matthew 28:3)

- Their number (Hebrews 12:22 and Daniel 7:10)
- Their speed (Daniel 9:21)
- Their warfare (Daniel 12)
- Their role (Hebrews 1:14)
- Their power (Daniel 6:22)

God's Glory Is Declared
in His Name,

YAHWEH-TSIDKENU, "THE LORD OUR RIGHTEOUSNESS"

Read Jeremiah 6:1–6

*This is the name by which
He will be called: "The
LORD Our Righteousness."*
(Jeremiah 23:6)

L ike a team that had traded away all its high draft picks of
the future, the kingdom of Judah was heading toward
disaster. It had good kings and bad kings, reformations and
counter-reformations. But overall, Judah was headed morally
and spiritually downward. Even the priests and prophets were
corrupt, falling into the same moral depravity as the heathens
around them. Political unrest, oppression, and violence
abounded. The day of *Yahweh's* grace had almost expired.
Jeremiah predicted the invasion of Jerusalem by foreign armies and captivity for God's people. Yet, all was not lost—for
ultimately Jeremiah predicted a great King in the line of David

would sit upon the throne of a restored Israel. His name would be *Yahweh-Tsidkenu* or "The LORD our Righteousness."

Modern man conceives of God as holding a scale upon which He balances our rights and wrongs; however, they never know how many good deeds are enough to outweigh the evil deeds they have done. They have good reason to worry, for deep inside they *know* they do not measure up to the standards of a Holy God. "How can a mortal be righteous before God?" Job asked (Job 9:2). Paul answers in Romans 3:10, "There is no one righteous, not even one." He concludes, "For all have sinned and fall short of the glory of God," (Romans 3:23). It is abundantly clear that no man is capable within himself of standing righteously before a holy, just, and perfect God. Our God is satisfied with no less than perfection, absolute obedience, and righteousness — 100 percent of the time! He will *not* overlook our sins, for the wages of sin is death (Romans 6:23)!

But *God* has done something to satisfy both His holiness and His justice. *He provides the righteousness!* Jesus Christ is the Righteous One of God, sent to live a perfectly righteous life before us and to die in payment for our sins! The Righteous One suffered for the unrighteous (1 Peter 3:18)! "God made Him who had no sin to be a sin offering for us, so that in Him we might become the righteousness of God" (2 Corinthians 5:21)! Can you even imagine such a thing? Never in our wildest dreams could we imagine that a perfectly righteous God would become the sin offering for sinful humans, and give salvation free of charge to all who put their trust in Him!

The great error of Israel (and of America) was that the nation refused God's offer. We seek to present to God our own righteousness — of which we have none (Romans 3:10). All who attempt to make themselves righteous are hopelessly lost in sin. No good deeds, religious rituals, gifts to worthy causes, or other deeds will suffice to pay for sin. May we stop trying to be righteous and accept the righteousness of *Yahweh-Tsidkenu* on our behalf!

Meditation Time-Out

1. How do you see yourself in relation to God?

    • Righteous on my own merits and qualified for heaven.

    • Better than most, probably qualified for heaven.

    • Some good, some bad points; hoping for heaven.

    • Not too good, probably will go to hell.

    • Absolutely a bankrupt sinner, deserving of hell.

2. How does God see you in your own righteousness?

    • Isaiah 53:6

    • Isaiah 64:6

    • Romans 3:10

3. When we accept Jesus' sacrifice on the cross in payment for our unrighteousness, how does God see us?

    • Hebrews 10:14

    • 2 Corinthians 5:21

4. According to the following verses, who does God justify (count as righteous)?

    • Romans 3:26

    • Romans 4:5

    • Romans 10:4

5. Praise God for providing the absolute righteousness of Jesus Christ for us!

God's Glory Is Declared
in His Name,

YAHWEH-SHAMMA, "THE LORD IS THERE"

Read Ezekiel 43:1–9

"And the name of the city from that time on will be: THE LORD IS THERE."

(Ezekiel 48:35)

G ary Anderson was a theological student from Axtell, Nebraska, who became a two-time Olympic champion. In both 1964 and 1968, he won the free rifle competition which required 120 shots at three hundred meters at a thirty-nine inch target with a bull's-eye less than four inches in diameter. In other words, it was like shooting a bullet through an apple from three football fields away! After the 1968 games, the twenty-nine-year-old Army lieutenant/minister told reporters he intended to keep shooting, "because I think it's important for a minister to be actively involved in what people are doing."[31] Obviously, Anderson felt it was imperative to *be there* for people who have needs he could meet.

Our God is always there for His people who have needs. Another of His names tells us so. The name *Yahweh-Shamma* is found in the last verse of Ezekiel, an Old Testament prophet who spoke to God's disobedient people. Deported from Israel to Babylon with other captured Jews in 597 B.C., Ezekiel had a vision of the glory of God departing from the midst of God's people (Ezekiel 10) and of the destruction of Jerusalem and the Temple because of Israel's abominable sins. In 586 B.C., this prophecy was fulfilled, and the remaining Jews were enslaved. Fourteen years later, Ezekiel uttered his last prophecy to a people of broken spirit and repentant heart. His message became one of restoration and hope as the glory of God returned to Israel (Exodus 43:1–9). The name *Yahweh-Shamma* (The LORD is there) was most encouraging to a sin-sick and forgiven people, for it demonstrated the loving concern and nearness of a God who would never finally and completely forsake His people.

Our God is a holy God, a God of discipline and chastisement of His erring children. He will not *wink* at sin in His people. But He is the God who is there, to restore and strengthen His people after He has "spanked them."

Yahweh-Shamma is our assurance that He will never forsake us (Hebrews 13:5), no matter how dark the day or severe the discipline.

Meditation Time-Out

1. Israel went on with their religious *system* without even knowing that the glory of God had departed. They had *religion* without a *relationship* with God! How often do you go through *forms* of religiosity (prayers, communion, church attendance, etc.) without really making *contact* with God? If He were to leave, would you

even notice? May our religion become a real relationship with a loving heavenly Father.

2. Study these verses. What do they reveal about the New Testament relationship between God and a believer in Jesus?

- Revelation 3:20
- Hebrews 12:5–7
- Hebrews 13:5
- Romans 8:37–39
- Philippians 1:6

God's Glory Is Declared
in His Name,

YAHWEH-ROHI, "THE LORD, MY SHEPHERD"

Read Psalm 23

*The LORD is my shepherd,
I shall not be in want.*
(Psalms 23:1)

S eldom has one man demonstrated the loving concern for
another that Gale Sayers showed to teammate Brian Piccolo. Sayers, a black man from Kansas University, and Piccolo, an Italian from Wake Forest University, were roommates
and best friends on the Chicago Bears' 1969 squad. That year,
Piccolo was tragically stricken with cancer, and Sayers spent
hours by his side. Gale would return early from games to get
to the hospital to encourage his friend. When he was presented
the George S. Halas Award as the most courageous player in
pro football for the 1969 season, Sayers had this to say:

"You flatter me by giving me this award, but I tell you
here and now that I accept it for Brian Piccolo. It is mine

tonight; it is Brian Piccolo's tomorrow. . . . I love Brian Piccolo, and I'd like all of you to love him too."[32]

Think of having a friend who loves you even more than Gale Sayers loved Brian Piccolo. That is exactly what every Christian has in the God of the universe! The name *Yahweh-Rohi* designates Him as the loving Shepherd who feeds His flock of tired, hungry sheep. In Psalm 23, called the "Shepherd's Psalm," David reviewed a life of stormy trials, a life filled with passion and warfare. He took great comfort in the thought that the great Shepherd always "restored his soul" after the storm. The word *Rohi* is further translated *companion* or *friend,* expressing the idea of "an intimate helper who shares life together." No other name of Yahweh has the tender connotation of *Yahweh-Rohi.* While His other names reveal His awesome holiness and majesty, the designation *Shepherd* reveals God's condescension to walk with and guide mortal, sinful creatures on this earth. Isaiah says of the Lord, "He tends His flock like a shepherd: He gathers the lambs in His arms and carries them close to His heart; He gently leads those that have young" (Isaiah 40:11). Ezekiel reveals the tender, loving care given by the true Shepherd of His people (Ezekiel 34:11–16) in contrast to the false shepherds who cared only for themselves (Ezekiel 34:1–10). Good shepherds in the land of Israel live with their sheep and call each by name. The sheep know the voice of the shepherd. A shepherd protects his sheep from thieves and from preying animals. He leads them to rich pastures and to fresh, pure water.

The Lord Jesus Christ is beautifully personified by the name *Yahweh-Rohi.* "I am the Good Shepherd," He said (John 10:11). He knows His sheep and they know Him (John 10:14). He laid down His life for His sheep (John 10:11, 15). No one forcefully took His life, for He laid it down willingly (John 10:17–18). His sheep will follow Him, for they realize He is

Lord. They will never perish, for He holds them in His hand (John 10:27–28).

The Good Shepherd knows our peculiarities, our frailties, and our weaknesses. Yet He loves and leads us. Surely goodness and love will follow us all the days of our lives, and we will dwell in the house of the Lord forever (Psalms 23:6). Thank you, *Yahweh-Rohi*! Thank you, Jesus!

Meditation Time-Out

1. From Psalm 23, list all the verbs that tell what *Yahweh-Rohi* does for His sheep (see verses 2, 3, 4, and 5).

2. Read John 10:1–30.

   • Does the Good Shepherd drive His sheep or lead His sheep (see verses 3–4)?

   • Why do the sheep not follow a stranger (see verse 5)?

   • What has Jesus the Good Shepherd, done for His sheep (see verses 11 and 15)?

   • Did Jesus tell the Jewish people plainly that He was Messiah (see verses 24–25)?

   • Why didn't the Jews believe Jesus (see verse 27)?

   • What do Jesus' real sheep do (see verse 27)?

   • What promise did Jesus make to His sheep (see verses 28–29)?

3. Imagine living in a violent, stressful world if there were no Shepherd to help you. How can you influence those who have rejected the Good Shepherd to come to Him?

God's Glory Is Declared
in His Name,

ADONAI,
"MASTER OR
OWNER"

Read John 13:1–17

> *You call me "Teacher"*
> *and "Lord," and rightly*
> *so, for that is what I am.*
> (John 13:13)

E ddie Feigner was a master of fast-pitch softball. He toured the United States with his four-man team under the title "The King and his Court." Eddie was clocked in his prime at 118 miles per hour, and he could make the ball rise, drop, curve or knuckle. He could deliver the ball from behind his back, through his legs, or from second base and still strike-out good hitters. In 8,500 career games, Eddie lost only 1,012 — with only a shortstop, first baseman, and a catcher! He once won 187 games in a row, and he struck out over 120,000 hitters in his career. Eddie deserves his reputation as *lord* of softball.

The title *Adonai* occurs some three hundred times in the Old Testament. It is almost always plural and possessive

169

(Lords'), confirming the idea of the Trinity. Psalms 110:1 is a good example. David writes, "The LORD [*Yahweh*] says to my Lord [*Adonai*]; 'Sit at my right hand until I make your enemies a footstool for your feet.'" In the New Testament, Jesus Christ refers this great promise to Himself (Matthew 22:41–45)! Truly, *Jesus* is both Lord (Master) and God! Occasionally, *Adonai* is used of men and is translated "master," "sir," "lord," or "owner." When used of men, it is always in the singular.

The name *Adonai* signifies ownership with perfect right of rulership over all men. Man is responsible and accountable to the Lord of the universe. The Lord has a definite claim upon man's loyalty, obedience, and service. Abraham, himself a lord over numerous others, acknowledged this truth in addressing God as "Lord God" (*Adonai-Yahweh*) in Genesis 15:2 (KJV). Moses, in protesting his inadequacy, refers to God as *Adonai* (Lord) in Exodus 4:10, 13. The LORD reprimanded for his reluctance to be used for God's purpose, for our Lord (Master) never asks us to attempt anything for which He has not equipped us! Isaiah was given a vision of the Lord (*Adonai*) and His majesty during a time of national tragedy (Isaiah 6:1). Ezekiel uses the name *Adonai Yahweh* some two hundred times, revealing that God claims lordship over all people of the earth, whether they acknowledge Him or not! Gideon, Daniel, David, and all others who refer to Yahweh as *Adonai* acknowledge Him as Master and themselves as servants.

In the New Testament, Jesus is called *Lord* and *Master* hundreds of times. Nathan Store says, "Lordship meant complete possession on the one hand, and complete submission on the other."[33] He is the *possessor,* the *owner* of all who trust Him by faith. We are His servants, totally submitted to His every desire. Some people maintain that a person can accept Jesus as Savior of their souls but reject His authority over their daily lives and decisions. But when you accept Christ as

Savior, you also get a new Lord (Master)! You may not acknowledge His Lordship, but He is Lord anyway! Eddie Feigner may have been a lord of softball, but Jesus Christ is Lord of all! He *will* rule your life! If you fail to submit, He will lovingly discipline you to conform you to His image! Why not make it easier on yourself and yield completely when He speaks? Doesn't the One who saved you for all eternity deserve control of your days on earth? *He* is *Adonai. He* is Lord!

Meditation Time-Out

1. If Jesus is Lord and you trusted Him as Savior, doesn't it stand to reason that He will take over your life?

   • What kinds of problems have you avoided because you submitted to His Lordship?

   • What problems have you caused yourself because you have rebelled against His authority?

2. How does the Lord treat His subjects in John 13:1–7? What does Jesus teach us about leadership in this passage?

3. According to Matthew 22:44, what is the destiny of the enemies of the Lord? Compare this verse with Philippians 2:9–11. Praise the LORD!

GOD'S GLORY
IS DECLARED
IN JESUS

Read Philippians 2:1–11

Therefore, God exalted Him to the highest place and gave Him the name that is above every name, that at the name of Jesus every knee should bow, in heaven and on earth and under the earth, and every tongue confess that Jesus Christ is Lord, to the glory of God the Father.

(Philippians 2:9–11)

N ame your favorite professional team sport: baseball, football, basketball, hockey — all have high-priced talent. More and more, these athletes are represented in contract negotiations with the owners by agents. The job of an agent is to speak for his client and to bring about agreement where there has been disagreement, especially in money matters.

The name *Jesus* means *Savior*. In fact, the reason God
named Jesus as He did is because He came to save us from
our sins (Matthew 1:21). When a person trusts the Lord to
save him, Jesus becomes the *agent* on that person's behalf before God the Father! There is *no other name* under heaven
given to men by which we must be saved (Acts 4:12). There
is *one* mediator between God and man (1 Timothy 2:5). He is
unique. He is Lord above all! Every knee must bow before
him! Jesus said, "Anyone who has seen Me has seen the Father" (John 14:9). When Jesus appeared to John on Patmos
(Revelation 1:12–18), His appearance revealed the very character of God. His robe spoke of His absolute authority; His
white head and hair of his purity; His blazing eyes of His
penetrating discernment; His bronze feet of His power to tread
upon evil; His voice like rushing waters of the urgency of
everything He utters; His sword of the powerful sharpness of
His Word; and His brilliant face of His glory!

Jesus is the Christ (Messiah), the Anointed One of God for
whom the Jews looked so long, only to reject when the Father
presented Him! Both Psalm 22 and Isaiah 53 give vivid de-
scriptions of the suffering of Messiah for the sins of the world.
Matthew 26:59–68 reveals the injustice of his accusers, the
lies with which they slandered him, how they spit in his face
and slapped him. Matthew 27:26 records his flogging, a
Roman practice that left the victim's back in ribbons of flesh
and often exposed the internal organs. Psalm 22 records how
men scorned, despised, mocked, and insulted him. His bones
were dislocated from their sockets, and his strength melted
away as His hands and feet were pierced on the cross (verse
14–18). Isaiah 53:1–2 records the pitiful misunderstanding of
the people because of His seeming insignificance. The Messiah who came was not the Messiah they expected, so they
rejected and hated Him. Verses 4–6 reveal that Jesus died as a
willing substitute for the sin and guilt of those who crucified
Him, as well as for all mankind. Verses 7–9 reveal that Jesus

was totally innocent and submissive to the will of God. Jesus died a criminal's death, though He had done *nothing* wrong! It was for *our* transgressions that He died. The Jews thought that Jesus was smitten because of His own wrong, but God laid upon Jesus the wrath that *we* deserve! Jesus was obedient to death, because He was paying for *our* sins. He died in *our* place. What a sacrifice!

Jesus predicted His own suffering when He said, "the Son of Man must suffer" (Mark 8:31; Luke 9:22). He predicted His betrayal (Mark 14:41), His trial and judgment (Mark 9:31; 10:33), and His death (Mark 9:9; Matthew 17:9). He predicted the three days in the grave (Matthew 12:40) and the resurrection (Mark 9:9). Jesus knew why He came and where He was going. What a Savior He is! Jesus is the Lamb of God (John 1:29) who perfectly fulfills the picture portrayed by the countless animal sacrifices of centuries. Jesus is the last Adam, who restores the life lost when the first Adam fell (1 Corinthians 15:22, 45). He is Immanuel, "God with us" (Matthew 1:23). He is both the Good Shepherd (John 10:11), and the Lion of the tribe of Judah (Revelation 5:5) who will devour His enemies! He is the Prince of Peace (Isaiah 9:6), and there will be no peace on earth until He returns to rule with a rod of iron (Revelation 19:15). He is the very Word of God (John 1:1–2, 14; Revelation 19:13) who created everything, took on flesh to buy it back from the curse of sin, and will one day take absolute authority over everything and everyone! He is the Alpha and Omega, the First and the Last, the Beginning and the End (Revelation 22:13)! And He is coming back to reign!

Meditation Time-Out

1. Picture the suffering of Jesus as proof of His love for you. How does the way He loves you differ from the shallow love of men?

2. Some people say God is *narrow-minded* for proclaiming Jesus as the *only* way of salvation. They criticize God for not doing anything about world conditions, as if He is to blame. Who has the right to set the condition of salvation?

3. Whose world is it anyway?

4. What *has* God done about the sin of the world?

5. Jesus Christ hung crucified and unashamed between heaven and earth for you. How does His love relate to your commitment to unashamedly stand for Him in school? In your work? In athletics? In worship and praise at church?

END NOTES

1. Greg Boeck, "Elway still ponders big leagues," *The SUNDAY Tennessean,* January 25, 1987.
2. J. I. Packer, *Knowing God* (Downers Grove, IL.: InterVarsity Press, 1973), 75–79.
3. Stephen Charnock, *The Existence and Attributes of God* (Minneapolis: Klock and Klock Christian Publishing, 1969), 72.
4. Ibid., 189.
5. Ibid., 155.
6. Arthur W. Pink, *Gleanings in the Godhead* (Chicago: Moody Press, 1975), 46.
7. Charnock, 190.
8. Millard J. Erickson, *Christian Theology* (Grand Rapids, MI: Baker Book House, 1983) Volume 1, 280.
9. Pink, *Gleanings in the Godhead,* 46.
10. Charnock, 140.
11. Peter Vecsey, *Coaching and Training Times,* (Cleveland, OH: Ross Laboratories).
12. Bill Glass and Mike Koehler, *The Commitment of Champions* (Dallas: Bill Glass Evangelistic Association, 1984), 25.
13. Ibid., 45.
14. Ibid.
15. Noah Webster, *Webster's Encyclopedia of Dictionaries* (New York: The Publisher's Guild, 1956, Second Edition).
16. Ibid.
17. Paul Kurtz, *The Humanist Manifesto II* (San Francisco: Prometheus Books, 1973), 3.
18. Ibid.
19. Erickson, *Christian Theology,* 287.
20. Curry Kirkpatrick, "Giant Killers," *Sports Illustrated* (June 19, 1989), 43.
21. Arthur Blessitt, *Glory* (Hollywood: Blessitt Publishing, 1988), 13–14.

22. *Our Daily Bread*, Radio Bible Class, Grand Rapids, MI.

23. *Nashville Banner*, April 18, 1987.

24. Andrew Jukes, *The Names of God in Holy Scripture* (Grand Rapids, MI: Kregel Publications, 3rd printing, 1980), 95.

25. "Last-Second Shot Gives Fort Hays Second Straight Title," *NAIA News*, April/May 1985, Volume 34, No. 5, 22.

26. Nathan Store, *Names of God* (Chicago: Moody Press, 1944) 68.

27. "Does Anyone Remember Who Came in First?," *Focus on the Family with Dr. James C. Dobson* (Pomona, CA: January 1987), 14.

28. Store, 78.

29. Store, 99.

30. Ibid.

31. David Wallechinsky, *The Complete Book of the Olympics* (New York: Penguin Books, 1984), 384.

32. Jeanne Morris, *Brian Piccolo: A Short Season* (New York: Dell Publishing Company, 1971), 163.

33. Store, 45.

ABOUT
THE AUTHORS

E lliot Johnson is a college baseball coach and assistant professor of physical education. He has held the position of head baseball coach at Trevecca College in Nashville, Tennessee, Taylor University in Indiana, and Great Bend High School in Kansas. He is the founder/director of Winning Run Foundation, a non-profit organization established for the purpose of publishing athletic-related devotional materials.

Elliot Johnson presently resides in Antioch, Tennessee, with his wife, Judy, and two sons, Todd and Benjamin.

Al Schierbaum is a part-time professor in the Religion Department at Dallas Baptist University, assistant baseball coach (pitching), and current chaplain for the university.

Al Schierbaum graduated from Dallas Baptist University in 1982 and then went to Criswell Bible College and obtained a Master's degree in Biblical studies. Al has coached Athletes in Action teams (both USA West and USA East) for the past two summers. With these college baseball squads, he has toured the U.S. and many foreign countries on mission oriented programs. He presently lives in Dallas, Texas.

The typeface for the text of this book is *Times Roman.* In 1930, typographer Stanley Morison joined the staff of *The Times* (London) to supervise design of a typeface for the reformatting of this renowned English daily. Morison had overseen type-library reforms at Cambridge University Press in 1925, but this new task would prove a formidable challenge despite a decade of experience in paleography, calligraphy, and typography. *Times New Roman* was credited as coming from Morison's original pencil renderings in the first years of the 1930s, but the typeface went through numerous changes under the scrutiny of a critical committee of dissatisfied *Times* staffers and editors. The resulting typeface, *Times Roman,* has been called the most used, most successful typeface of this century. The design is of enduring value to English and American printers and publishers, who choose the typeface for its readability and economy when run on today's high-speed presses.

Substantive Editing:
Michael Hyatt

Copy Editing:
Darryl F. Winburne

Cover Design:
Steve Diggs & Friends
Nashville, Tennessee

Page Composition:
Xerox Ventura Publisher
Printware 720 IQ Laser Printer

Printing and Binding:
Maple-Vail Book Manufacturing Group
York, Pennsylvania

Cover Printing:
Weber Graphics
Chicago, Illinois